A WOMAN OF VISION

A True Story of Courage,
Determination, and Vivid Blindness

Written by
Joanna Rivera Stark

Joanna Stark (signature)

As told by Betty Clark Mong

CONTENTS

$\mathscr{F}$OREWORD

"$\mathcal{S}$hoot for the moon. Even if you miss, you will be out among the stars." This is just one of the many inspirational messages Betty Clark Mong delivered to our new eye doctors at the opening day of their education program at the ophthalmology department of the Doheny Eye Institute and the Keck School of Medicine of the University of Southern California. She also said, "Set high goals and standards. Do not be discouraged if the eye treatment or surgery for your patient fails. Do not give up."

These messages, especially coming from Betty—who experienced the highs of restored vision only to suffer the lows of sudden vision loss—were very important words of advice, not only for our trainees but also for our faculty and staff. The ophthalmology department trains students who have completed their internships and then spend three years of residency to become full-fledged ophthalmologists. As chairman of the department, I am certain Betty's message of hope and perseverance is an important one for all of us to remember as we treat our patients and try to prevent and cure blindness. For ten years, Betty was the main attraction at our opening-day ceremonies. There was always a mixture of tears and smiles when Betty spoke to us.

She has also been the main attraction for many other gatherings of medical personnel, organizations, and the general public, not only for vision-impaired people but also for anyone who is faced with seemingly impossible challenges in life. Her philosophy of sensitivity and good sense permeates her lectures. She was clearly an apt student of human nature, and her inspirational messages resonate with everyone, regardless of personal situations and life experiences.

I first met Betty when I became a member of Braille Institute of America's board of trustees in the mid-1970s. Betty had been working at the Institute since 1971. Like everyone who has ever met or worked with Betty, I was immediately impressed with and inspired by her commitment to others with sight problems, especially those with severe forms of blindness. Her work at Braille Institute as a community relations coordinator and later as an inspirational speaker and consultant became an important part of the institute's culture and programs. She soon also became my patient. As explained in chapters 2 and 3, she suffered sight loss from complications of juvenile arthritis and was severely visually impaired as a child and adult.

A Woman of Vision documents the extraordinary life and times of Betty Clark Mong. She has lived a unique, interesting, and exciting life with many experiences, including enrolling as the first blind student to be mainstreamed into the Los Angeles School District, which demonstrated her early tenacity in overcoming the legal blindness. Her life path has even included a friendship with a Las Vegas mobster.

I was particularly involved with Betty and Stuart when she became a patient of mine as noted in chapters 12 and 13. It is during this time that I witnessed first hand her inner strength, determination and resolve.

When Betty experienced events that would have ruined the lives of other people—she developed a platform to become an even more inspirational and sensitive person and speaker. She was more attuned to the importance of relationships and compassion for individuals with illness or disability, especially blindness. Her public speaking became legendary, and she soon emerged as a valued spokesperson, not only for patients with vision-related disabilities but also for others faced with challenges and barriers in daily life.

A Woman of Vision is a wonderful tribute to the transformational power of courage, perseverance, and compassion. Betty has inspired me personally to become a better physician for my patients, a better leader and teacher for my students, a better husband and parent, and a better person. You, as a reader of this book, will also be touched, inspired, and made a better person.

Ronald E. Smith, *MD*

Professor and Chairman
Doheny Eye Institute
Keck School of Medicine of the University of Southern California Department of Ophthalmology

$\mathscr{P}$ R E F A C E

$\mathscr{I}$ have lived during one of the most extraordinary periods of world history. I have witnessed transportation go from steam engine trains to Boeing jet airplanes; education leap from textbooks to Macbooks; medical advancements grow from penicillin to stem cells; and technology bound from telegraphs to the Internet.

It has been a grand adventure to navigate through my own learning and development as the world around me has raced toward our high-speed technological age. Yet even with all the advancements, some things stay the same: wars still kill people, disease still spreads, and the human psyche still swings from diabolical to saintly. But what never, ever changes is the need for compassion and understanding to enable us to survive as a species.

At various times during my life I have been faced with obstacles that threatened to stop me from becoming the person I wanted to be. At an early age I learned *not* to accept "no" and "you can't" as reasons why I shouldn't try new things. I am often amazed that I have somehow been allowed to live, love, and enjoy such a rich and fulfilling life.

Now more than ever, it is important for me to make a meaningful contribution to my community in gratitude for the love and support I have been given throughout my life. I believe the best way for me to do that is to share the culmination of my life's work and my philosophy of *sensitivity and good sense* that puts compassion and understanding to work. This is especially important in the area of implementing ways to assist and enjoy friendships with those who may be physically or mentally different from the majority of our population.

I have given compassion and understanding to many who I have met through my life's journey. I have received more compassion and understanding than I ever could have imagined. There are many opportunities for all of us to educate ourselves and to learn how to lend support and to encourage others toward independence and success. This is why I want to share my story.

Betty Clark Mong

$\mathcal{A}$CKNOWLEDGMENTS

$\mathcal{OW}$e are so grateful to the many people who have contributed to and supported the creation of *A Woman of Vision* in one way or another. Each provided a thread that, when woven together, helped, as actress Patty Duke said, bring Betty's story "into the light."

At first Betty did not want to have any personal acknowledgments. "What if I forget someone? That would be awful! You just do your own, thanks." With a little prodding and at the last minute Betty decided that she would try to remember as many people as she could, and she would hope for forgiveness from those who were important to her that she forgot to include.

Betty thanks her family, especially her beloved and now departed parents, Bela and Tom Clark. Their love, sacrifices, and tireless perseverance kept her alive and gave her countless opportunities and experiences she would not have otherwise had.

Betty had wonderful friends throughout her life, and she recalls a few with deep appreciation: Jeff and

Kay Wilson, Benni Stephens, Betty Buchannan, Marie Wicks, Michael Landes, Diana Hamel, Howlett Smith, Gene Shaw, Susan Hegge, Michael Cosgrove, and Roger Bearman.

Braille Institute was the source of great colleagues and treasured friends: Jay Hatfield, Sue Berkman, Sally Jameson, Les Stocker, Russell and Marion Kirbey, Jennifer Chambers, Gina Fields, and Norm, the dearest volunteer and person she had the pleasure to work with.

Betty's dear friend and confidant, Jennifer Chambers, volunteered to transcribe *A Woman of Vision* into braille. It was a daunting task that she undertook with expert skill, perseverance and a great sense of humor. Mere words cannot express our gratitude for her work, transcribing, editing, overseeing a web page and for her friendship treasured by both Betty and me.

Special thanks go to Betty's medical team, who were not only her physicians but her friends as well. In no particular order, they are Dr. Michael R. Gato, Dr. David B. Ko, Dr. John K. Schofield, Dr. Melvin A. Gonzalez, Dr. Gary Annunziata, Dr. Timothy Richardson, Dr. Bruce Chisholm and Dr. Javed Siddiqi. Last, but by no means least, is Dr. Ronald E. Smith. Betty says, "He changed my life by giving me an amazing gift and wonderful opportunities to share my story. Words will never be enough to thank this kind and wonderful doctor and friend."

Segovia Signature Living was Betty's last home. She thanks the staff and residents for their interest and support and in particular Nicholas Eames and Anke Ramero.

We are so grateful for earlier readers who provided invaluable wisdom and technical advice: Chuck MacKinnon, Rachel Horton, Risca Edlin, Karl Stober and Barbara Foster.

We also thank these talented photographers: Janel Pahl for Betty's cover photo and the photo of Betty and Stu in the epilogue, Maile Klein for the author's photo, and Randall Richards for his image of Howlett Smith in the interior of the book.

We especially thank Anna "Patty Duke" Pearce, Denise DuBarry-Hay, Dr. Ivan Misner, Audrey Moe, Laura Little, and Kim Waltrip for their valuable assistance, contributions and encouragement during the writing of this book.

I, like many authors, could not have completed this book without the love and patience from the family I neglected so often during this process: my husband, Ron Stark; daughter, Raya Rivera; sister and brother-in-law Leigh and David Greenhaw; and stepsons Kevin Stark and Kris Stark and their families. I, like Betty, had remarkable parents, Maki and Chester Hunt, who gave me everything and more.

And finally, I thank my lucky stars for Betty Clark Mong, who chose me to write her story. It has been a passionate and amazing adventure.

Joanna Rivera Stark

$\mathcal{D}$OWN THE $\mathcal{R}$ABBIT $\mathcal{H}$OLE

Writing with Betty
By Joanna Stark

$\mathcal{D}$ uring the summer of 2012, my husband, Ron, and I were living near Coeur d'Alene, Idaho, to escape the relentless heat of our Coachella Valley, California home. In August, I received a surprise phone call from a long-lost friend, Betty Clark Mong.

I met Betty years ago through Braille Institute in Rancho Mirage, California, and later I was in the audience when she spoke at a Rotary Club luncheon about her life and work at the Institute. I, like many others, was captivated by her charm, her wit, her sense of fun, and her elegant appearance. A year later, when Ron and I were considering a subject to write about for an upcoming book, we thought of Betty. We wrote and submitted a manuscript about Betty's very successful life. The story was selected to be included in the book *Masters of Success*, part of Business Networking International's *New York Times* and *Wall Street Journal* bestselling *Masters* series.

During our reunion phone call, Betty said, "I have been looking for you all over. Your phone number has changed, and I didn't know how to get in touch with you." She told me in detail all the steps she had taken to find me and then came to the point of why she was calling. "I want you to write a book about my experiences and about sensitivity and good sense."

She also explained that she and her husband, Stu, had been in a terrible accident a few years back, and through excellent medical care and months of physical therapy, they had survived. However, Stu had died recently, and she was having serious health problems. Therefore, there was some urgency to get this book completed.

Several things went through my mind after the phone call. Would there be enough interesting material to fill a book? Would Betty be able to complete the project if we started, or was it just a momentary whim? Then there was the Morrie factor. I love the book *Tuesdays with Morrie* by Mitch Albom, the true story of the reunion of a sociology professor and his student years later. Their fourteen Tuesday visits resulted in a wonderful book of wisdom and life lessons. My father, not unlike Morrie, was a wise and gregarious sociologist and that might have been another contributing factor for my love of the book.

A romantic scenario of Betty and me as the female versions of *Tuesdays* ran through my head. I could easily imagine us having weekly meetings, sitting quietly, with pearls of wisdom springing forth as we chatted and sipped tea. That made the project almost irresistible. I decided to visit Betty in her Palm Desert, California, home to further explore the possibility of writing her story.

When Ron and I returned to the Coachella Valley in late September, I immediately went to see Betty. She was living in an apartment in an upscale independent-living complex. On the phone she instructed me that the door would be unlocked and to come right in when I arrived. As I entered her room, I announced myself so she would know who was there. I took a quick glance around and recognized the sofas and chairs from the home she had shared with Stu. Sitting on the edge of an adjustable, single bed with a tea cart alongside her was Betty. She was still lovely and beautifully dressed, with her hair coiffed and makeup applied. The total effect was pure elegance.

We began our conversation by catching up on our lives and then phased into the idea of the book. Betty explained that losing her husband had been devastating. All she wanted to do was have her story told and then "go be with Stu." Her resolve on both counts was more than evident, and my heart ached for her. I agreed to write a chapter to see if she liked the style enough to proceed together.

Two days later, I returned with a chapter in hand and read it to her. She was very enthusiastic about what I had written and excitedly listed all the things she would talk about in the next few days. "I want to have the book finished by the end of the year," she said.

"Betty, I would like to see it finished that quickly too, but the reality is that it takes at least a year to complete a project like this."

She responded, "I may not have a year, so let's get busy."

We were off and running. We settled into a fast-paced schedule of work with my fifty-mile-round-trip visits four to five times a week. Each visit I pulled a chair up to the side of her bed and she would pick up where she left off by recalling another event or adventure. Then I raced back home to translate her memories into words that represented what she had revealed to me from her heart, soul, and spirit. We had considered taping the sessions, but fiddling with the equipment was distracting for Betty and got us off course. So she talked, and I typed on my laptop.

It soon became very evident that Betty and I were having a completely different experience than that of Morrie Schwartz and Mitch Albom. We had a difficult period of adjustment in which Betty fired me twice and

I thought of quitting just as many—if not more times. It was mostly the pace Betty was concerned about. We were not moving fast enough through the book, and I was concerned we were moving too fast. She could be headstrong and outspoken, wanting always to have the last word, but I could match that with my quiet stubbornness.

Finally, we settled into a compromise, and by mid-November of 2012, we had four chapters under our belts. During each visit, I was astounded by some event or enchanted by a memory she recalled. After the visits, I often spent hours researching the time period and events Betty referred to. She had a speaker's promotional package that contained news articles, a biography, a DVD of one of her talks, and a long list of awards and recognition. But I needed far more information to substantiate all we had been talking about.

One day Betty mentioned she remembered that there were some old photos and scrapbooks in her storage unit. This was exciting news, and I could not wait to see what she had. About a week later, I walked into the apartment, and there were two suitcases and three boxes of photographs, articles, awards, scrapbooks, and memorabilia piled up on the floor. It was like Christmas morning. I got on my knees and peeked into the boxes. "Oh, my gosh," I told Betty, "this is like going down the rabbit hole into Betty Land."

We tackled the new information a box at a time. I described photos and read articles to Betty, and off we would go into another period of her life. Organization of the photos and documents was essential, so I bought a box of Ziploc gallon bags and began to sort through everything. For days, my dining-room table and any other surface I could find was covered with piles from this treasure trove of information. I scanned photos and documents we would use and returned the originals to Betty.

Then we began to write in earnest. I arrived at Betty's apartment every other day at ten. I pulled my chair up alongside her bed, where I could hear her best, and put my computer on my lap. Betty would lie back with her right arm behind her head and begin talking. I took notes and asked questions until we had enough "meat" for writing. We usually finished between two and three. On occasion we would wander down the hall to the restaurant in her building and have a working lunch, but more often than not we worked right through.

My study at home was the "rabbit hole". I surrounded myself with copies of Betty's photos, taped to the closet's sliding doors. My desk was littered with research notes, and stacks of chapter drafts lay on the carpet. I wrote mostly while sitting on the sofa in front of my desk. I put my feet on the footstool and my computer on my lap and became totally immersed in Betty's history for hours at a time.

If I had a question, I would call her on the telephone. If she remembered something, she would call me. I often answered jokingly by saying, "Betty, don't bother me. I am down the rabbit hole," to which she would always reply with peals of laughter.

Betty traveled through her life over and over again as we edited and reedited, draft after draft. During one session, in sheer frustration, she sputtered, "I don't want to talk about that little girl Betty anymore. I am so tired of her." She was very clear about what she liked and didn't like and often made astute suggestions for rewording.

I knew there were times when Betty was in great discomfort caused by medical issues, but she never complained. As she began to talk, a look of serenity would settle onto her face. It was as if the pain had disappeared, and she had moved to another plane. During these times, I wondered how so much courage, strength, and fierce determination could be held in such a tiny body. I also wondered how, when she was so physically weak, she always managed to have the last word.

In one session, Betty was talking about the things that constitute the foundations of a successful life. She compared it to the building of the pyramids in Egypt, saying, :When the pyramids were finished and the bright coats of paint were applied, they stood forever."

I interjected, "Betty, the pyramids aren't painted."

There was a pause, and she almost whispered, "They aren't?"

I could hear the disappointment in her voice, and I knew I had been the spoiler of a beautiful image of the pyramids she had had in her mind's eye for years. I felt horrible.

During another conversation, when we were discussing physical appearance, she said, "Every man I meet is handsome, and every woman I am introduced to is beautiful. That is just the way I see people."

I thought about that for a minute and said, "So, what you are telling me is that you have vivid blindness."

She laughed. "That is it exactly. In my mind I see such vibrant colors and beauty everywhere." Then I understood that she had the remarkable ability to imagine everything as beautiful until someone told her otherwise.

By December, the stress of our schedule was beginning to wear on both of us. I came down with a bacterial infection, and Betty was hospitalized with fluid on her heart. We both recovered and went right back to work, abandoning our families and friends. We worked on Christmas Eve and New Year's Eve, and we pushed right into 2013. During the ten months of writing, Betty was hospitalized five times, and I lost my mother, my aunt, and my stepfather. We were now so bonded in this single goal that we moved together through each challenge like Olympic hurdlers running shoulder to shoulder.

A friend noted that Betty and I were an odd pair. "You are quite tall, and Betty was delicately petite," she said. "Betty was blind, and you are, for the most part, deaf. You two are a generation apart, yet you act like sisters." Indeed, with all the time we spent together, we did feel like family. We learned each other's strengths and frailties. We cried together when we learned that both of us tragically lost husbands too soon. We shared secrets and laid our souls bare more than once. We told wicked jokes that made us laugh hysterically and talked about every topic under the sun.

We debated which was worse: my hearing loss or her sight loss. She felt my loss was worse than hers. "I could never live without being able to hear all the wonderful sound in the world," she said.

I, of course, replied, "And I could not live without seeing all the wonderful sights." We chuckled at the irony of it all.

Then she said, "So tell me about your *vivid* deafness."

We truly came to love and respect each other in a way that would not have happened if I had not gone "down the rabbit hole."

Going down the rabbit hole is a magical story in itself. It was a grand adventure of discovery and full of surprises. The longer we worked on the book, the less Betty talked of dying. Through it all, she gracefully moved from despair to joy. Her last wish–this book–was coming true. And though she lost love, she found love and security again in her devoted personal assistant, Roger.

Betty, like all of us, wanted to be accepted, unlabeled, for who she was in her heart. She worked all her life to prove that she was just like anyone else. But she wasn't. Betty was undeniably one of the most exceptional people ever to grace our planet.

Here is her story.

1

ℰSCAPE TO THE ℬEGINNING

*I*f I have learned nothing else in my ninety years on this planet, I have learned that the most powerful tool for survival is our ability to sustain the positive relationships we have developed throughout our lives. We react to, learn from, and imitate behaviors to which we are exposed. Linked together, these interactions nurture us, guide us, and shape how we travel from birth to death.

The most influential relationships of my life were with my mother and father. Their lives were not always easy, but as they moved from hardships to success, they gained knowledge and experience that enabled them to pass along invaluable gifts to my brother and me. These were the gifts of sensitivity, tenacity, and most importantly, abiding love.

Oliver Twist could not hold a candle to the childhood suffering my father, Tom Clark, endured at the hands of those who were supposed to love and protect him. His mother, an immigrant from Norway, died when Tom was four years old. He was suddenly left alone with an abusive father whose rages included nearly daily beatings. With no one to protect him and nowhere to go, Tom had no choice but to bear the abuse as bravely as he could.

Tom's father, my grandfather, remarried a woman who was equally as cruel and took the saying "Spare the rod and spoil the child" to her very cold heart. It soon became clear that Tom's stepmother had no interest in raising another woman's child, so she and my grandfather left young Tom in an Iowa orphanage.

As you might imagine, life in an orphanage in the late 1800s was miserable. What should have been a safe haven for children was, by all accounts, a dangerous prison with the most vulnerable of inmates. Older and bigger children preyed on the younger, weaker ones. The staff often brushed away clinging children who craved attention, affection, and protection. There was overcrowding, filth, disease, physical and sexual abuse, and a lack of even the most basic educational experiences.

My father defied the survival odds of those who grow up in an orphanage in more ways than one. Physically he grew into a sturdy young man and emotionally he was filled with spirit, confidence, determination, and hope. But he knew he had to get out of there if he was ever going to have any kind of life— and the sooner the better. He had to escape.

So late one night, when he was fourteen years old, he snuck out of the orphanage and onto the streets. The streets were not much better than the orphanage. There were dangers at every corner—con artists, thieves, and drunks—but at least if you found a job and worked hard, you could have a better life. That is what my father dreamed of: a better life, a wife, a family, love, laughter, and a house with food on the table every night, and he was willing to work for it.

It was not long before Tom did have a job and a good friend, Lamar "Mac" McConnell. The two worked hard during the day and hung out together at night. One Saturday night, as they walked the streets deciding what to do, they passed by the Bell Telephone offices. Through the window they could see a young switchboard operator efficiently managing all the cords and plugs that connected callers. Mac began to jump around, flailing his arms in the air, trying to get her attention. She glanced around, making sure her coworkers weren't watching, and gave a little wave back.

Tom was dumbstruck by the petite, auburn-haired beauty with soft, hazel eyes. By this time, my father was a handsome, blue-eyed, dark-haired, strapping lad of five foot ten. He and the girl caught each other's eye for a moment, and she smiled then went back to connecting calls.

Tom turned to his friend and said, "Hey, Mac, I am gonna marry that girl."

Mac shouted back, "The hell you are! That's my sister!"

Despite Mac's initial protest, Thomas H. Clark and Bela McConnell married in their early twenties. They were very young and very much in love. They wanted to see the world and began married life by embarking on a grand adventure, traveling by bus through the Midwest and south to New Orleans. They got odd jobs along the way to finance their trip and found rooms in boarding-houses or small hotels.

My mother had never traveled so far south before, and she noticed that there were far more black people in New Orleans than she had seen in all of Iowa. She was immediately enchanted by the obvious differences and looked forward to befriending and learning more about them and their lives. But Bela noticed that every time she and Tom approached black people, they would move off the sidewalk. This became frustrating to her because she never had the opportunity to properly greet these folks and introduce herself to those whose skin and hair was so much darker than hers.

One day she'd had enough. She leapt off the sidewalk and followed a "Negro" couple, calling out, "Hello, hello. My name is Bela. I just wanted to introduce myself. What are your names?" The couple bowed their heads and kept on walking in silence.

My mother was crestfallen. "Tom," she said, "why don't they want to be friends?"

My father gently explained that things were different in the South. It wasn't that they didn't want to be friends; it was because they couldn't. It was far too dangerous. He said, "Some situations are just impossible to escape from. There are invisible chains that have a strong grip on those folks."

She sighed and shook her head in disbelief.

As time went on, my parents became aware of just how dangerous things really were in the South for non-whites in 1915. They learned that a white supremacy group, the newly reorganized Ku Klux Klan, based in Atlanta, Georgia, was deeply rooted in the South and rapidly spreading across the United States. Acts of terrifying violence against Jews, Catholics, African Americans, and immigrants left them fearing for their lives. My mother finally understood the depth of the dangers that the couple she had approached on the street faced.

It was an experience she never forgot and a story she repeated to my brother and me often during our childhood. For us, it was a glimpse of our mother's innocence and her practice of kindness to all throughout her life. It was also a beginning of her lifelong, deep concern for social justice. My father's desire for equality for all Americans was just as strong as my mother's. Together they lived through one of the most tumultuous and painful struggles our country experienced. They admired Martin Luther King Jr. and would have been pleased to know that, years later, America would choose an African American president based not on the color of his skin but on his extraordinary qualifications.

New Orleans is also where my mother discovered she was pregnant with me. Both my mother and my father were delighted with the news they would be parents. They thought they should probably return to Iowa to be close to family for the birth, so they gave notice to their employers and planned to head north a few weeks later.

The pregnancy was going well; my mother was healthy and feeling great. I was, by all accounts, growing into a healthy and very active baby, making my mother's tummy leap this way and that. One day my mother went to my father and moaned, "Oh my, Tom, I think we better start home now. This kid really wants out!"

Betty and her father, Tom

My parents made it home, and in 1921, I was born into loving arms. My arrival created the family my father had dreamed of all those years ago. While I was growing up, I loved listening to the stories my parents told of their romance and the adventures that led up to my birth and early life. The stories were great lessons of love and perseverance.

It was from my father that I first heard the word *escape* and from him I learned the most important thing about the art of escaping: what one escapes to is just as important, if not more so, as what one escapes from. My father escaped to the true beginning of his life.

2

MIRACLE

My mother and father began parenthood trying to keep up with a healthy and always-bouncing baby girl. I have been told that I began walking at about twelve months old, as most children do, and once I discovered what feet were for, I was off and running with my anxious, happy parents not far behind.

Although they were delighted to be in Iowa around friends and family, my parents found job prospects slim. My father had a difficult time finding full-time work, and the odd jobs were hardly enough to support a family. The newspapers were full of stories about opportunities in California, so my parents took what little savings they had and headed west to the growing, bustling city of Los Angeles.

Once there, they rented a little house and began to look for work but again found full-time jobs just out of reach. Although discouraged, they did not give up hope, and my father took whatever day work he could find while my mother managed the household and cared for me.

Betty and her mother, Bela

Just four months after we arrived in Los Angeles, my mother had what she said was the most frightening experience of her life. She was in the kitchen preparing dinner, and I was playing happily in the living room. She heard a loud, screeching cry from me that she had never heard before. She ran into the living room to find me facedown on the floor with my legs drawn up behind me. And I was unable to move from that position. She picked me up, and still my legs remained curled and cramped toward my backside. My father was called, and they raced me, still crying, to the hospital.

It took days to diagnose what had caused my condition. It was juvenile arthritis, an autoimmune and inflammatory condition that develops in children sixteen and under. Simply put, the body's immune system, which is supposed to fight off viruses, mistakenly attacks healthy tissues and cells. The resulting inflammation can cause permanent joint damage. Though it typically affects joints, it can also involve the skin, gastrointestinal tract, and eyes. Over the years several different types of juvenile arthritis have been identified, which helps in the diagnosis and treatment of the disease. In my case, the treatment was still in the early experimental stages and encompassed all forms of the disease.

The news was devastating to my parents. What were they going to do? They had a very sick child and almost no income to deal with the expenses that lay ahead. The treatments and physical therapy began, and ankle-to-thigh braces were put on each of my legs to encourage them to grow straight. I called them "hurts" because wearing them was terribly painful, especially in the beginning.

The doctors explained to my parents that I would never be able to walk normally again. The braces would be with me the rest of my life. Although my parents understood what was being said, they never accepted that prognosis. I would walk freely again, they said, because they were going to find a way to make that happen.

A series of exercises and treatments from other doctors and chiropractors began. One suggested a glass of orange juice followed by a glass of water every hour. Believe it or not, that did help a little, but what helped me the most physically and emotionally was a little wooden kiddie car my father brought home one afternoon. It was a tricycle with two wheels in the back and one in the front, and no pedals. I would sit on the car and move from place to place by pulling forward with the tips of my toes. Soon I was racing around the house at an alarming speed and enjoying every second. It was my only escape from the confinement of my braces, which held together my little, weak legs.

Betty on her Kiddy Car

At about this time, my father finally found a job demonstrating cake and pastry flour for Belford and Guthrie Mills, headquartered in Vancouver, Washington, with branches in Los Angeles and San Francisco. Initially he traveled quite a bit while my mother and I waited patiently for his return home from each trip.

My father developed his own fruitcake recipe while doing demonstrations in grocery stores around California. When he was home, he made fruitcakes in a local bakery, using his secret recipe, and brought them home to prepare for sale. My mother would take the bedroom door off its hinges, lay it on their bed, and cover it with clean paper. Then we would wrap each fruitcake in cellophane and tie it up with a pretty bow. My father would take these packaged fruitcakes around various California cities and towns to sell them to stores and bakeries.

One time Daddy offered to take me along while he made a delivery in the Los Angeles area, and I was thrilled that I got to go in the car with him on an important job. When we arrived, he parked the car directly in front of the bakery. Knowing it would be nearly impossible to juggle a stack of fruitcakes and a wiggly three-year-old with braces on her legs, he said, "You wait right here in the car. I will just be a minute. I will be able to watch you through the window, and you will be able to see me."

I was devastated. "No, Daddy, I want to go with you," I wailed. "Please, Daddy, please take me with you."

"Betty, I will just be a minute. Be a good little girl and wait for me here," he said firmly, and then he closed the car door.

Well, to me, that minute was more like an hour, and when he got back to the car, I was sobbing uncontrollably. "Betty," he asked, "what on earth is wrong?"

"You broke my heart, Daddy. You just broke my heart."

By the time we got home, my heart had healed, and I had a brand-new teddy bear.

My parents continued to consider every avenue for finding a cure for my arthritis, including spiritual guidance. Every week we attended the neighborhood Seventh-day Adventist church. One Saturday, our Sabbath, my mother reminded me to remove the little ring on my finger before church, because wearing jewelry was frowned on. I replied, "Jesus sees me wear this ring every day, and he hasn't said a word about it to me yet." So off we went to church, my parents shaking their heads and me wearing my little ring.

I enjoyed the services and especially liked the singing. I soon had many hymns memorized, and each week I sang more enthusiastically and apparently more loudly. The congregation took notice, and requests were made for me to sing a solo. So at the next service, my mother set me atop the grand piano in the sanctuary and accompanied me while I sang a couple of hymns. The congregation responded with much appreciation and requested more performances. Soon, and at age four, I was singing in churches all over Los Angeles while my mother accompanied me on the piano.

We were so poor during that time that Mama's threadbare taffeta dress hardly held together. She worried that the back of her often-mended dress would be visible to audiences while she played the piano, but that would soon change.

Word got around about a little blond girl with braces on her legs who could belt out a song, and a Los Angeles radio station invited me to perform live on one of their shows. What a thrill! It was there that I met the Beverly Hill Billies.

This was many years before television became a household fixture, so the Beverly Hill Billies I knew were *not* from the 1960s *Beverly Hillbillies,* the TV series most people are aware of. These Hill Billies were a popular country band of the 1920s and '30s that tried to convince people they were real hillbillies that had come down from a remote area of the mountains surrounding Beverly Hills. The members included Tom Murray, Ashley "Jad" Scraggins, Shug Fisher, Norman Hedges, Chuck Cook, and Len Dossey. Their theme song was "Red River Valley."

In the early days, before their fame and fortune, the Beverly Hill Billies and I were booked as singing acts for special events such as store openings, public gatherings, and programs. I was now making money and able to contribute toward our family expenses. During this time, I never felt I was being exploited, as people have often wondered. I loved singing and being able to perform before a live audience. I could not walk, run, hop, and skip like other kids, but I did excel at something very special, and I was helping my family.

The Hill Billies and I were invited by Aimee Semple McPherson to sing at the Angelus Temple in the Echo Park area of Los Angeles. Sister Aimee, as she was known, was a charismatic spiritual leader, minister, faith healer, author, radio personality and station owner, and social activist who founded the International Church of the Four Square Gospel. In the 1920s and '30s, she could draw crowds in the tens of thousands, and her three daily services at the temple included pageantry, large choirs, elaborate sets, and costumes—all in an auditorium that seated 5,300 people. She was the first woman to preach over the radio and the most photographed person of her time, and that propelled her to such fame that people came from all over the world to see her.

I remember what an imposing figure Sister Aimee was. She was tall, beautiful, and always elaborately dressed. The three hundred choir members wore white robes, and Esther Fricke was at the organ. Sister Aimee gave me beautiful silk dresses to wear when performing. Before each performance, she would call me on stage, and in a cloud of perfume, she would give me a huge hug.

A favorite song I sang at the Angelus Temple—one we knew would always bring the congregation to its feet—was "Open Them Pearly Gates."

My mother had a four-page promotional flyer printed with the sheet music for "That One Lost Sheep." The flyer was handed out after performances and included a list of ten songs I sang, along with a photo of me at age three and contact information for bookings. I was a very busy little girl.

One day my mother was returning home from grocery shopping when she saw a pair of red, patent-leather Mary Janes in a shoe-store window. Mary Janes were simple, flat-heeled, round-toed shoes with a strap that crossed over the top of the arch of the foot and fastened on the outside of the shoe. They were very popular when I was a girl, and my mother knew I would love them. But they were expensive, and it would be foolish to spend money on such a luxury for a child with braces who would probably never be able to walk in them. But the shoes were just my size, and there seemed to be something special about them. Her heart overruled her head, and she paid for the shoes and brought them home.

I could hardly believe my eyes when I saw them. They were the most beautiful shoes I had ever seen, and they were mine. I squealed, "Oh thank you, Mama! Hurry. Take off my hurts, and let's put on my new shoes." My mother removed the braces from my legs and strapped a shoe on one foot and then the other. Oh, they were such a beautiful, bright, ruby-red sight at the end of my legs! Without thinking, I stood up and walked across the room for the first time in almost four years.

3

YOUNG TRAILBLAZER

I did not start school at the age of four or five, as most of my peers did. From the time my juvenile arthritis struck at age eighteen months until I was six years old, all my parents' and my attention was directed at keeping me well. Endless doctors and treatments were needed to improve my health and abilities before attending school could even be considered.

I did have a lot of interaction with neighborhood children and typical childhood adventures, especially with the boy next door, Bobby. When he and I were about five years old, I had regained the use of my legs, and I was fully enjoying my mobility. So we planned what we expected to be an elaborate escape from parental tyranny. We announced to our mothers that we were running away from home, and to our surprise, they thought it was a splendid idea. They packed each of us a lunch.

Unknown to us at the time, our mothers watched from the kitchen window as we defiantly marched up to the top of the hill that was less than a block away. Once we got there, we were unsure what to do next. Our plan did not entail much more than walking out the door and to the end of our universe, which was the top of the hill, so we sat on the curb and ate our lunches. After the lunches were finished and we became bored with sitting on the curb, we decided it was best to return home so as not to further worry what we were sure would be our distraught mothers. In addition, there was the lure of the swing set and the safety of our own backyards. While it may not seem a particularly distinctive childhood experience, for me it was the beginning of relationships beyond those with my parents and medical personnel.

Only a few months later, at dinner, my parents discovered I could not see the food on my plate. Everyone had been so watchful for any recurrence of arthritis in my limbs that no one had realized my eyesight was failing. I was so used to adapting to all sorts of things that I had naturally adapted to the loss of vision without complaint. All we knew was that I could see only light, dark, and shadows.

This was so unexpected and frightening that my parents once again raced me to the doctor. With tests, they discovered that the arthritis had moved to my eyes and it was unlikely I would ever see normally again. I was left with between 2 and 3 percent vision. Another round of doctors and treatments began, and my family and I had to adjust to a new way of living to accommodate my sight loss.

During this time, my father began to take me to baseball games. The Pacific Coast League was one of the premier regional baseball leagues in the United States. The warmer climate on the West Coast allowed for a longer season, and with no major league teams west of St. Louis, these teams enjoyed almost major-league status. My father described the plays, and he and I would whoop and holler in the stands, eat Cracker Jack, and sing "Take Me Out to the Ball Game." Most importantly, we would have baseballs autographed after the games. It was great fun, and I still have a collection of baseballs from that era, along with wonderful memories of time spent with Daddy.

I had become a bright and precocious little girl, so when the time finally came for me to go to school, I was more than ready. My parents had learned of the Blind and Sight Saving School that was in a small wing of the Thirty-Second Street School near Shrine Auditorium in Los Angeles.

The Blind and Sight Saving School was established by the Los Angeles United School District in 1926 and was the first of its kind in the western United States. It provided regular classroom curriculums, classes for learning to read and write braille, and instruction and exercises to promote independence. Its principal, Miss Frances Blend, had begun with the school district as a substitute teacher. She was called to substitute in a classroom with one of the first blind students placed in a public school in the United States. Miss Blend developed a close academic relationship with the student and learned the needs and abilities of the blind. The experience motivated her to become one of the first advocates for education of the visually impaired.

My parents met with Miss Blend, and arrangements were made for me to be enrolled in the school. I would have an hour of bus and streetcar rides each way. Nonetheless, the program was a wonderful opportunity to have a well-rounded education and to be schoolmates with both visually impaired student and the general student population.

Every weekday morning, my mother would wake me, make a lunch, and help me get ready for the day. Then the two of us would walk to the bus stop to catch a ride to the streetcar line. We would get off the bus and wait for the streetcar that would deliver us very close to my new school. Once my mother dropped me off, she would board a returning streetcar, then a bus, and walk from the bus stop home. In the afternoon, she reversed the process and arrived just as school was letting out.

On one occasion, as we arrived at school, my mother realized she had forgotten my lunchbox, which left me with nothing to eat during the day. She dutifully returned home, picked up my lunch, turned around, and got right back on the bus and then the streetcar to deliver the box to me. Then she went home again until she made the trip once again to pick me up from school. That day she spent nearly six hours on buses and streetcars. She never forgot my lunch again, and I have never forgotten her endless devotion.

Even though the trips to and from school were long and tiring, being on the streetcar with my mother was a special time. We talked about my day at school, chatted with other passengers, and enjoyed the bustling sights and sounds of the city of Los Angeles. We even got some of my homework finished while being jostled through the streets.

In the 1920s and '30s, school curriculums included reading, writing, and arithmetic, along with social studies, science, and geography, which were generally incorporated into our reading textbooks. My report cards were divided into two sections: citizenship and scholarship. Citizenship had five components: obedience, dependableness, courtesy, cleanliness, and thrift (which was respect for the property of others and recognition of the value of time). Scholarship included effort, reading, English, social studies, music, home economics, and typewriting. I had a wonderful teacher throughout my years at Thirty-Second Street School, Ruth Farley. She encouraged and guided me to become a successful student, and we remained good friends until her death.

I also had braille classes that I really enjoyed. The newly established Universal Braille Press in Los Angeles was developing a library of braille books, and it was a great source of reading material for students and the visually impaired public.

Braille, as you may know, is a system of writing developed in 1824 by a fifteen year old Frenchman, Louis Braille, who lost his sight at the age of three in an accident. Braille consists of small, rectangular cells made up of two columns with three dots in each column. The dots are embossed or punched into a thick paper, making various combinations within each cell to represent a letter or number. A slate and stylus or a machine called a braillewriter that functions much like a typewriter are used for personal writing. Braille systems vary from language to language, and American Braille has grades or levels of writing. Grade 1 is a basic letter-by-letter transcription. Grade 2 uses abbreviations and contractions. Grade 3 is a nonstandard, personal, shorthand version.

J. Robert Atkinson, a Montana cowboy who lost his sight in 1919, learned to read and write braille. He found that there were very few books in braille available and began to transcribe hundreds of books, including the King James Version of the Bible, into braille. His family members took turns patiently reading each word of a book while he laboriously transcribed day after day. With the help of John and Mary Longyear, Atkinson established the Braille Universal Press and was instrumental in passing the 1931 Pratt-Smoot Act, which provided funds to print and distribute raised-print media through the Library of Congress Services for the Blind.

I learned to read and write braille quickly and enjoyed trips to the Braille Universal Press to see the latest books available for students. Today I still use braille for personal note taking and to keep my daily calendar and address book up-to-date.

Betty and Mrs. Atkinson

The other students in the Blind and Sight Saving School had varying degrees of vision loss, and some had no vision at all. But that did not keep any of us from being aware of what was cool. Then, like now, there was a fashionable style of clothing unique to the times. Girls wore dresses or skirts and blouses to school. No girl would ever dream of wearing pants or jeans to school, let alone shorts, for heaven's sake. A popular hairstyle for girls at that time was to have their hair cut in a bob with bangs across the forehead right above the eyebrows and shingled along the nape of the neck. The hair was cut straight on the sides, just below the earlobes. Boys wore shirts, often ties, trousers with socks, and polished leather shoes. No sneakers. Boys' haircuts were neat, cut close on the sides, and slicked back at the crown with a Vaseline-type of hair balm called pomade.

It was particularly important for those of us in the Sight Saving School to be well groomed and fashionable so as not to be confused with those who were mentally or physically unable to care for themselves. We were proud of our abilities and knew first impressions were critical. We were just great kids who were smart and caring and who enjoyed music, dancing, games, and movies, just as our peers did.

The school had classes for elementary and middle school students. Everyone assumed that I, like all other students with sight loss, would go to Polytechnic High

School, where there was a specialized program and a Braille room. One day, our principal, Miss Blend, pulled me aside and said, "Betty, high school is just around the corner for you. I want you to go to a regular high school. You are ready to become more independent, and it will make all the difference in the world when it comes time for college and jobs. With your personality, social skills, and intelligence, you will do well in a public high school, and I will not have it any other way." My parents whole-heartedly agreed. But I was a little nervous.

Miss Blend went to visit Mr. Sniffin, the principal of John Marshall High School, and persuaded him to allow me to attend the school. In September of 1935, I was en-rolled in the school, which was in the Los Feliz District of Los Angeles, near the Hollywood Bowl and the Greek Theater. I was to become the first visually impaired stu-dent in the Los Angeles School District to be completely mainstreamed into the general student population. Mr. Sniffin met me at the door on my first day and introduced me to the staff in such a way that I knew he would be not only my principal but also a friend. Miss Blend went on to found the Frances Blend School: A Public School for the Blind, which is now part of the Los Angeles Unified School District.

The John Marshall High School was about a mile away from our home. Initially, my parents drove me to and from school, but soon classmates would drive up to our house, honk their horns, and yell, "Hey, Betty, come on! Hurry up or we'll be late." I would go flying out the door with books in hand and pile into the waiting car.

High school was a particularly happy time in my life. I made friends easily, the schoolwork was interesting, and my grades were good. Other students and friends read assignments to me, and my teachers gave me oral exams, so I had very few adjustments to make. I participated in the Glee Club's Gilbert and Sullivan musical productions and the Girls Athletic Association. Respect and courtesy for all were highly valued traits at that time, and so I never experienced any of the discrimination or bullying that you hear of today. I was just one of the gang who liked hanging out with friends, giggling with the girls, and teasing the boys.

Life at home was good too. My parents' business was growing, and we all worked filling and packaging confection orders. We attended Seventh-day Adventist services on Saturdays, and I continued to sing in churches and for special events. My darling little brother, Tommy, was growing by leaps and bounds. Every time I looked at him, I remembered the moment of pride when I was allowed to hold him in my arms during the car ride home from the hospital. I was ten, and he was *so* cute. Watching him grow into a handsome boy was a source of joy for the entire family.

I graduated from high school in 1939 and attended the Seventh-day Adventist Pacific Union College in Napa Valley of Northern California with the goal of becoming a speech therapist. There I discovered I had a gift for public speaking. After a year at Pacific Union, I decided to transfer to the Berlitz School in Los Angeles, where diction was taught. Diction is the art of speaking and enunciating clearly so that the audience understands each word. Pronunciation, tone, and emphasis were all skills incorporated into the program. I was not sure how I was going to be able to use these skills, but I was confident that someday I would be able to put all those hours of practice to good use.

I was happy to be back in Los Angeles and reunited with friends and family. I jumped right back into working with my family, going to classes, and spending time with friends.

It seemed like the good times would last forever.

4

THE USO AND THE SPRIG

*M*ost of us can remember exactly where we were when a catastrophic event happened, such as the assassination of John F. Kennedy and the plane crashes into the World Trade Center. Those events stop us in our tracks and make us realize that we all were suddenly catapulted into an unexpected event that changed how we lived. My first experience with such an event was December 7, 1941.

It was a lovely day, with temperatures in the mid-seventies, so my friends and I headed to the beach in Santa Monica. The beach was bustling with all the usual activities, and we settled onto the sand with our blankets and picnic lunches, expecting to have a long, leisurely day of fun in the California sun.

The ten of us—five girls and five boys—were all in our early twenties. Romances were budding, schooling was completed for the most part, and our futures lay ahead alluringly. We were young and attractive, and on that day, we were full of ourselves, laughing, teasing, running in the sand, and jumping in and out of the water without a care in the world. All the while, a dark disaster was taking place in another part of the same beautiful ocean we were enjoying.

It was in the earliest part of the afternoon when the atmosphere at the beach began to change. At that time I had about 2 to 3 percent vision, and I could distinguish forms of people and their movements. It seemed to me that everyone on the beach began moving much slower and seemingly without destinations. Then we heard someone shout, "The Japanese have bombed Pearl Harbor. Our ships are all sinking."

At first we were not sure what they were talking about. The vendors on the beachfront had radios that they turned up full volume so the beachgoers that gathered around could hear the news as it was being broadcast.

The Japanese had attacked the United States without warning at the naval base at Pearl Harbor that was located on the south side of the island of Oahu. The attack began at 7:55 a.m. and went on until 9:45 a.m., lasting 110 minutes and killing 2,335 US servicemen and wounding another 1,143. Sixty-eight civilians were also killed, and thirty-five more were wounded.

At the time of the initial news broadcasts, no one knew the extent of damage to the US ships or the number of lives lost. We did not have television yet, so we relied on the words and tone of voice of the announcer to help us understand what was happening. We could only imagine the horror. The newscasters made it very clear, in their fast-paced, blaring reports, that this was catastrophic. We were stunned, and all kinds of thoughts raced through our heads. *Are the Japanese now on their way to the West Coast?* We hugged each other, ran home to the comfort of our families, and later learned that our beloved country, the United States of America, had been drawn into the Second World War.

The next day, all five of the boys who had been on the beach with us enlisted in the US military. In that same circle of friends, Gene Copenhagen and Esther Mussulmen decided to marry before Gene was shipped off to the Pacific. By the time he left, Esther was pregnant with their baby boy.

All our lives changed dramatically as the country rallied to do all it could to protect our shores and our servicemen and women abroad. We did not complain. We did what we had to do.

I had never been so aware of national unity or felt such personal patriotism as I did during that time. I most certainly wanted to do my part in the war effort. Almost all American women immediately went to work filling the jobs men left vacant when they went off to war. New jobs were created in factories that produced airplanes, machinery, munitions, parachutes, and other supplies needed to protect our country. The Red Cross needed volunteers to roll bandages and assemble emergency kits.

The United Service Organizations (USO) needed thousands of volunteers to provide services, programs, and live entertainment in centers across the country. What most people recall about the USO during that time was the thousands of volunteers that staffed centers in hundreds of American cities to hand out coffee and donuts to young men and women going off to war.

If I could have joined the service, I would have been the first in line, but with my limited vision, that was not possible. It seemed the best place for me to volunteer was the USO, and I threw my heart and soul into it.

The USO was established in 1941 and was so new that many servicemen and women were not aware of what it did. One of my first jobs was to let soldiers know about the programs available to them and to provide rides to the USO in our area. My aunt, Virginia, who was only five years older than I, drove a Willys jeep through the streets while I hailed down servicemen and offered them a lift to the USO. For the most part, the guys jumped right in, happy for the lift. However, one fellow only reluctantly accepted our offer and sat nervously at the edge of his seat the entire ride. We never knew if he was more afraid of two gregarious young women picking up hitchhikers, Virginia's driving, or going off to war.

Many families, including ours, opened their homes to servicemen and women during Thanksgiving and Christmas and held special parties and box-lunch socials throughout the year. The socials were particularly popular. Girls would pack lunches in boxes they had decorated. These were placed on tables, and the soldiers would bid on the boxes (usually with money provided by local families). The highest bidder would receive the box and eat lunch with the girl who prepared it.

Holiday guests from the USO at the Clark home

A couple of years into the war, I was serving coffee and donuts at the USO when a young man came through the line and said, "Hi, Betty. You might not remember me, but I was at your house for Christmas two years ago. I am home on leave for a couple of weeks now, and I am so glad to run into you here again. I have something I want to show you." He placed a little, dried sprig from a pine tree in my hand. "I snapped it off the beautiful Christmas tree at your house and put it in my wallet to remind me of home and the wonderful afternoon I had at your house. It has been with me through some really tough times in this war, and when I thought I could not stand one more minute, I would take it out and hold it. This little bit of your Christmas tree has given me such comfort in the times I needed it most. So I hope you don't mind that I broke off this little bit from your tree. I am really glad I found you here today, because I wanted to thank you and your family for sharing your home and your hearts."

I was so touched by his story that tears filled my eyes. I handed him back the sprig, and he put it back in his wallet. I gave him a hug, and he moved down the line, leaving me with a wonderful memory that would last a lifetime.

5

LOST

On Saturday nights, after volunteering at the USO, my girlfriends and I would go home and change into our dancing shoes and head straight for the Hollywood Palladium on Sunset Boulevard in Los Angeles.

The Art Deco Palladium opened in 1940 with Frank Sinatra and the Tommy Dorsey Band in a ballroom that could hold four thousand people. During the war years, radio broadcasts from the Palladium featured Hollywood stars who took song requests from servicemen and women. Those broadcasts increased the popularity of the Saturday-night dances there, and the ballroom was the most exciting place to be in all of Southern California. It was a great escape, if only briefly, from the terrible news from the war's front lines.

My parents insisted that I look my best at all times. "Your vision is no excuse for not taking care of yourself," they would say. My hair was to be in place, my clothes clean and pressed, and my shoes shined. As I got older, I learned how to apply my own makeup in a way that looked stylish, not garish, and to fix my hair in fashionable styles. My attention to my appearance was not motivated by vanity, as some might think. It was always because of an intense desire to have people see me as a capable, confident, intelligent, and attractive woman, not to dismiss me as a "handicapped" person who was disheveled and dull-minded. Attention to daily grooming was my way of escaping those stereotypes and becoming a role model for others.

On one particular Saturday night, I dressed in a plaid taffeta skirt with a black blouse and placed a big bow in my shoulder-length, light-chestnut hair. It just felt like it was going to be a special night, and I wanted to look my very best. My girlfriends complimented my outfit as we went off, skipping arm in arm, to the Palladium, anticipating an evening of big band music and lots of dancing.

When we arrived, the music had started, and servicemen and women were pouring in, looking for the perfect dance partner. Up in the balcony was an army air corpsman who told his buddies, "See that cute girl down there with the bow in her hair? Look out! She is mine. I am going to ask her to dance." So Stuart Mong came down from the balcony, walked over to me, and asked, "May I have this dance?" The band had just begun its next song, "As Time Goes By." I took his hand as he led me out to the dance floor, and we danced as if we had been dancing together for years. The romantic lyrics seemed to be written just for that moment.

It's still the same old story,
A fight for love and glory,
A case of do or die,
The world will always welcome lovers as time goes by...

Stuart Mong

We danced several more dances together and with others that night. When the night was over, we went our separate ways and back to our daily lives. At the time I didn't know if he had been shipped overseas or if I would ever see him again. I hoped so.

My friends and I continued our Saturday-night outings at the Palladium, where we always had a good time listening to the bands and dancing with the guys. Then one evening one of my girlfriends whispered in my ear, "Betty, guess who is strolling across the dance floor with a big smile on his face?"

"I can't guess," I said excitedly. "Who is it?"

Then a deep male voice I would never forget said, "It is me, Stu Mong."

I couldn't believe it. I had thought I'd never see him again. He took me in his arms and twirled me onto the dance floor, and we danced and talked the night away.

Stu and I enjoyed each other's company and went on dates when we could. We always had so much to talk about. A few weeks later, he told me he had received new orders. He was being sent to San Francisco to attend German language classes at Berkeley. This was in preparation to be part of the occupying forces in Germany at the end of the war. I was heartbroken that he would be so far away. The day before his departure, we met again. Suddenly shy, we left many things unspoken, saying our good-byes with a hug and handshake.

I first met Stu's sister, Leslie, an operatic singer, when she and their mother came to Los Angeles for a visit. We hit it off and became good friends. Leslie enjoyed her stay in California and decided to return some months later to visit Stu in San Francisco, and she invited me to come along. How could I say no? I had not seen Stu in such a long time, and the opportunity to see him again was like an unexpected gift, especially when times were so uncertain.

Stu and I were happy to see each other, and Leslie, knowing we needed some time together alone, went off to see the sights of San Francisco. Stu and I found a cozy alcove in a student lounge on the Berkeley Campus and chatted away, catching up on the events that had taken place since he had left Los Angeles.

Stu told me about the intensive German language program he was enrolled in and how charmed he was by his instructor. She was a German woman who had cleared an extensive background screening process that allowed her to stay in the United States to teach the course. He also told me that she had been a world champion fencer and kept her students' attention with fascinating stories of her adventures. I told him about how much my family's confection business had grown and how busy we all were, trying to keep up with orders from the military bases.

After a couple of hours of chatting back and forth, there was a long pause in the conversation. That is when

Stu got up out of his chair, walked over to me, bent down, and planted the most delicious and memorable kiss of my life right smack on my lips. It was like a lightning bolt had hit me. He said nothing, walked back to his chair, and sat down. Together, in a dreamy silence, we waited for Leslie to return from sightseeing.

The visit was over, and I reluctantly left San Francisco, still dizzy from that kiss, wondering if I would ever see Stu again. In a few months, he had finished with his course and was fluent in German. So the US Army, in all its wisdom, sent him to France, though he knew only very basic French.

I returned to Los Angeles and went back to work in my parents' confection business and continued volunteering at the USO. I watched servicemen and women come and go, served gallons of coffee, handed out hundreds of donuts, and secretly hoped Stu Mong would come walking through the door.

Not until I received a long letter from Leslie in which she mentioned Stu had found a girlfriend in France did I realize it was not to be. It stung a bit, but I cannot say I was completely heartbroken, because it was about the same time that a tall, dark, and handsome young man walked into my parents' confection shop. Still, there was a sense of loss, and Stu seemed to be forever in the back of my mind and always in a pocket of my heart.

6

EIGHTEEN YEARS

*M*y parents' confection business grew rapidly during the 1940s. Their clients included the military Post Exchange (PX), Walt Disney Studios, Del Webb, and a host of celebrities. My mother arranged a variety of confections in trays, baskets, and gift boxes that were so popular, people were given numbers for service as they lined up outside the shop to make their purchases.

As the business grew, so did the need for more workers. My father hired a tall, dark-haired, good-looking, young man named Al. Al was a weight-lifter and as handsome as they come. He was also a hard worker who often spent nights in the shop when things got really busy. Al endeared himself to everyone and eventually worked his way up to supervisor.

I was also working in my parents' business, waiting on customers, taking telephone orders, and typing them up for pickup, for delivery, or to be shipped directly to the customers. I was quick and efficient, and when Mrs. Coe called in an order, I said, "Yes, Mrs. Coe. Of course, Mrs. Coe. Thank you, Mrs. Coe. We will have that sent out right away." Later that afternoon, we received a curt telephone call. "This is Mrs. Coe, *not* Mrs. Cow." I could have died right on the spot! We lost Mrs. Coe as a customer, and I learned to double-check every little detail in the orders that came in.

It seemed inevitable that sparks would fly between Al and me. I was the boss's lovely daughter, and he was the strong, handsome, charming right-hand man to that very same boss. We dated for a few months, and a real romance developed. I thought the world of him. He was the kind of man who is there if you need him, whether it be for family, a friend, or a neighbor. He helped people move, painted their houses, and did emergency odd jobs. He would do anything for you. It was a side of him that I adored, so when he proposed, I did not hesitate for a second to say yes.

We married in 1945 and had a big wedding at the Ambassador Hotel in Los Angeles. The hotel was also the location of the famed Cocoanut Grove nightclub, where film and music celebrities frequented. I had to pinch myself many times because the romance and the wedding made me feel as if I was living in a fairytale.

My parents had come a long way from the early years of their marriage. Now their daughter was getting married in a beautiful hotel with 450 guests as witnesses. As I look back, I realize that while I took it all in stride, my parents must have been pinching themselves too, while secretly taking pride in their elevated stature at that point. Against all odds, they had become very successful.

Betty and Al

Al and I rented a little one-bedroom apartment on the tenth floor of a building on Sixth Street, not far from West Lake Park in Los Angeles. Al loved dogs, and one afternoon he burst into the apartment and announced, "I don't drink and I don't smoke, so I want to keep this little puppy. I named him Duke." From behind his back, he brought around the cutest little St. Bernard puppy. I was flabbergasted and reminded him that we were not allowed pets and that it would be real hard to hide a puppy that would grow into a two-hundred-pound St. Bernard. It broke Al's heart, but he took the puppy out to his parents' home, and they raised and cared for Duke until he died.

While my brother and I were growing up, we had a variety of animals as pets. We had a dog and a cat as well as a white duck named Donald and his best friend, a soft, fluffy bunny, to name a few. I loved animals, and although I never felt the desire or had the time for a guide dog, I did like having dogs as household pets.

Al struck up a friendship with musician and actor Curt Massey, who had a ranch near San Diego. Curt and Al were avid hunters, so they spent hours tromping around with their guns and a pack of Weimaraner dogs that Curt raised. When a new litter was born, Curt gave us an adorable puppy that we just had to keep. It was clear that we could not stay in a tenth-floor apartment with a rambunctious puppy, so we moved out of the apartment and into a place not far from my parents' home.

Al and I continued working in the business, and my father offered him a partnership in Tom Clark Confections. Now we were busier than ever, and time seemed to fly by. We did find time for socializing with family and friends. Al had a great family that I loved, and I truly enjoyed the times we spent together. It was a very happy time for us...or so I thought.

My happiness made me disbelieve and ignore problems that were clear to others from the beginning of our marriage. There were signs that Al was not being faithful. It seemed he had girl friends everywhere. There was his best friend's wife, a coworker's girlfriend, a woman as old as his mother, and even my alterations lady. This did not go unnoticed, and he was caught in the act more than once. Al was chased by an outraged, knife-wielding husband and was hunted down by a bunch of men who showed up at the apartment threatening to kill him. Girlfriends called our house surprised, then furious, to discover he was married.

About five years into the marriage, Al joined the Masons and attended all the events necessary to maintain his membership. At about this time he began drinking. He realized he had a problem from the beginning and would muster up the courage to try to stop. On three different occasions, he went to the hospital to dry out. I encouraged him to stay dry. I supported him. I stayed with him, hoping things would get better.

Things did not get better, and after eighteen years of marriage, we finally sat down for a long talk and decided things were no longer working for either of us. Our situation would never be good again, and divorce was the only option. We did not tell anyone about our decision. There was a certain stigma attached to divorce in the 1950s that embarrassed us, and there was the crushing weight of the sense of failure. So until the very last minute, we attended family functions and parties as a couple. I let Al file for the divorce and did not ask for anything.

Al had several other later relationships. He eventually married a woman and had a son, but he could not escape what the years of drinking had done to his body, including what was likely cirrhosis of the liver. I remained close to Al's family through the years, and they kept me informed about his condition.

When I heard he was seriously ill, I went to see him. I was shocked to see that he was just skin and bones. I sat on the edge of the sofa where he lay, and we talked. He took my hand in his and said with pained and sincere eyes, "Those first five years I was married to you were the happiest of my life." I hoped with all my heart that those words were true.

Not long after my visit with him, his family called and informed me that he had died alone in his home following a fall. I was devastated that he had suffered and his life had ended so sadly.

For years I felt sad and guilty that I had not been able to save Al, that I was somehow responsible, that I might have done more. I wished I had known about Alcoholics Anonymous and Al-Anon then. These wonderful organizations were just gaining momentum around the country, and I was simply not aware of them. What I have learned since from friends who have gone through the Alcoholics Anonymous twelve-step program is that I could not have saved Al, no matter how hard I tried. He had to save himself.

Even so, I believe my last conversation with him was comforting for both of us. He had the opportunity to apologize and tell me he truly had loved me. Also, it allowed me to shed those thoughts of inadequacy and to finally put to rest the heartache of a lost love and the shame of a failed marriage.

7

A WORLD APART

While I continued my USO volunteering and working in my parents' confection business, Stuart Mong worked toward completing his US Army language studies at Berkeley. It was wartime, and our duties pulled us in different directions. There was really nothing we could do to change that. Our communication seemed to fade naturally as we became immersed with our own responsibilities and lives. Still I could not seem to forget Stu, so I just tucked away the memories in the back of my mind.

Stu had grown up and gone to school in the small town of Scottsbluff, Nebraska. His favorite subjects were French, music, and art. He loved the violin and practiced religiously. And with those same hands that were so talented with a bow and strings, he discovered he could shape hunks of clay into beautiful sculptures. By the time high school graduation came around, Stu had a pretty good idea of what he wanted to do with the rest of his life.

In 1937 Stu enrolled at the Kansas City Art Institute, where he studied painting and sculpture. He took summer classes at the University of Colorado and then transferred to Bethany College in Lindsborg, Kansas, where he received a bachelor's degree in fine arts. He kept up his violin skills and played in the first violin sections in the University of Colorado and Bethany College Symphony Orchestras.

Stu was a dedicated student and dreamed of one day visiting the mecca for artists: Paris. Little did he realize his dream would soon come true but not quite as he had envisioned it. The Second World War broke out, and he enlisted in the US Army Air Corps in 1941. The army was particularly interested in Stu's ability to learn languages, and after basic training, he was sent to the University of California in Berkeley for the two-year, specialized army training program to learn German.

Stu's language instructor was an attractive, blond German woman named Helene Mayer who was an Olympic fencing champion as well as an educator. She won the gold medal in Amsterdam during the 1928 Olympics, finished fifth in the 1932 Olympics in Los Angeles, and remained in the United States to study at the University of Southern California. She planned to return to Germany to compete in the 1936 Olympics to be held in Berlin. But in 1933 the Nazi government notified her that she had been expelled from the fencing team because of her Jewish lineage. Her father, a doctor, was Jewish and her mother Lutheran.

Once 1936 rolled around, German-Jewish athletes were invited to compete for Germany but were not allowed back into German society. Despite protests from her American friends and colleagues, Helene returned to Germany to compete because she feared repercussions for her family if she refused. She won a silver medal in her last Olympic competition in Berlin. All in all, she won a silver Olympic medal and a gold Olympic medal, two Italian national championships, two European championships, four world foil championships, and eight US women's foil championships. After the 1936 Olympics, she returned to the United States, and the US Army approached her to teach German classes.

Helene Mayer

Helene was an excellent but strict teacher who understood that her students' lives might one day depend on how well she taught them. She was also very lively and personable, which kept the young soldiers engaged in their studies. Fräulein Mayer and her students became very close and kept in touch until her death from breast cancer at age forty-three. In 1968 Helene was named one of the top one hundred female athletes of the twentieth-century.

After passing the language course, Stu reported for duty, joining the Ninth Air Force and the First Allied Airborne Army in England. This unit helped spearhead the invasions of Normandy and Southern France, and it was in France that Pfc. Stuart Mong made a bit of international news. It seems that Stu was on guard duty at a troop carrier base in France when, in the wee hours of the morning, he heard two men approaching the post. He raised his carbine and ordered them in French to halt. It was at that time the men shed their overcoats to reveal the uniforms of German paratroopers.

Stu quickly switched languages from French to German. The Germans told him they had escaped from an American prison train a week earlier and were hungry and tired. Stu escorted them to headquarters, where he locked them in a shower room and called the MPs. The prisoners were happy to be captured and fed, and Stu was happy to finally put his German language skills to work. So that is how Pfc. Stuart Mong made his big capture of two Nazi escapees. A dispatch from the base sent a humorous story of the incident to the *Stars and Stripes* newspaper, and it found its way into several US newspapers.

Stu was later stationed near Chartres, France, as a cartographer and French interpreter. The city was famous for its beautiful cathedral, which had been spared from the Second World War bombing, as well as its churches and museums. Stu, with the heart of an artist, filled an album full of photographs of the cathedral and other sites around Chartres. He also met a lovely young French woman named Josette. They had a two-year romance that did not survive his return to the United States. Josette would not leave Chartres and Stu longed to go home.

After his discharge from the army, Stu dove back into his studies. He took specialized courses at the University of Colorado and earned a master's degree in art from the University of Oklahoma. Not long after, he took a position at Bowling Green State University in Ohio, where met and married a journalism instructor at the same institution.

Soon after, the Milwaukee Art Institute in Wisconsin offered—and Stu accepted—a position as building and installation supervisor. It was a time of personal growth for him. He learned the operation of an art museum inside and out. Two years later he became the director of the Oshkosh Public Museum in Oshkosh, Wisconsin. In each community he continued to play the violin in symphony orchestras and create his own art. His sculptures and paintings were exhibited around the country. Stu was an avid reader and collected an impressive library of books dealing with Native American art. He particularly admired the art of his good friend Amee Blue Eagle, who was an internationally known artist from the 1930s to the 1950s.

Stu

Friends and colleagues described Stu as soft-spoken, self-contained, scholarly, and kind. I recognized those traits in the young soldier I met at the Palladium just after the war broke out. There was something about Stu that made him stand out from all the rest: a warm, broad smile, a silly sense of humor, an intelligent mind, and a gentle touch. These are all the reasons I never forgot Stuart H. Mong. I always secretly hoped I would see him again, and he always seemed to always be in the back of my mind. I knew I had to find him again. But how?

My very young aunt, Virginia, and I were only five years apart and had been friends through thick and thin. She was my confidant, my pal, and my partner in just about any crime. She knew all my secrets, shortcomings, and attributes and did not hesitate to jokingly use anything against me.

Virginia and I traveled the country together for my speaking engagements. The moment we arrived in a new city or town, I would ask her to look and see if she could find the name Stuart Mong in the local phone book. It got to the point where we would open the door to a hotel room, and as we stepped in, she would say, "I know. Stuart Mong." But nothing ever turned up.

Then one day, while I was vacuuming the living room carpet, it just popped into my head. Leslie. Curtis Institute of Music. Philadelphia. Stu's sister had studied voice at the Curtis Institute of Music in Philadelphia.

I turned off the vacuum and went right to the phone. I called the institute and asked if they might know her whereabouts.

The operator said, "We might have her current address in our files, but I am sorry, I can't give you that information. If you would like to leave your number, I will pass along your information to her."

"Oh, would you please?" I answered, and I gave her my number.

Two weeks later, Leslie called. "Oh my gosh, Betty! How are you?"

I was so delighted to hear from her and learn she was happily married and living in Wisconsin. I filled her in on all the things I had been doing, and the conversation finally got around to Stu. "Leslie, next time you talk to Stu, tell him to give me a call if he is ever in California."

She replied, "Next time I write to Stu, I will include your number."

I hung up from my conversation with Leslie and immediately called Virginia. "Virginia, guess what! Guess what!" I shouted.

"What?" She sounded almost frightened.

"It's Stu! I found Stu!"

"Praise the Lord above!" Virginia said with a long, exhausted sigh.

A week had passed since my conversation with Leslie. Then two. No call from Stu. Then it was one month after another and no word from Stu. I could accept a note that said, "Good to hear from you, but I am involved" or "I don't plan to be out that way anytime soon, but if I ever do, I'll give you a call." But no answer at all? I was so disappointed. I guessed it just was not to be.

A year later Stu was unpacking some boxes he had kept in storage from his last move. On the top of inside of one of the boxes was a stack of mail he remembered throwing in at the last minute. He sat on the floor and thumbed through the envelopes. *Mostly junk mail anyway,* he thought. Then he found a letter from his sister. *Oh my gosh! Leslie would kill me if she knew I never read her letter,* he thought. He ripped open the envelope and began to read the year-old newsy letter. *Holy cow! Betty Clark. The cute little Palladium princess!* He went right to the phone.

8

$\mathcal{T}$ H E $\mathcal{W}$ I L D $\mathcal{S}$ I D E !

$\mathcal{T}$he 1920s and '30s were filled with highly publicized criminal activity. Prohibition and the Great Depression turned many ordinary people to thievery, bootlegging, and even murder to keep food on the table. Wild West criminals like Jesse James, Cole Younger, the Dalton Gang, and Billy the Kid gave way to Bonnie and Clyde, Al Capone, John Dillinger, American mobsters, and European syndicated gangs like the Mafia.

Dime novels, newspaper stories, and radio programs often sensationalized crime and romanticized the criminals. The excitement of G-men and the mob chasing each other and shooting it out was certainly an entertaining distraction from the misery of poverty and unemployment. Gangsters and their molls (girlfriends) were glamorized to the point that, when I was a young girl, I secretly thought being a moll might be something nice to aspire to. The women were beautiful, dressed in pretty clothes, got lots of press, and seemed full of power and passion.

The truth is I knew real men with lawless backgrounds. One was a family friend we all adored. My parents spent many evenings having dinner and conversations with Emmett and Julia Dalton, who lived just down the street from us. My memories are mostly of the Daltons being included in activities, as were other neighborhood friends. They were childless and doted on my baby brother, who was adorable beyond words and responded to their attention in ways that enraptured them even more.

Emmett Dalton was the only surviving member of the infamous Dalton Gang. The Dalton brothers were lawmen gone bad. Emmett, being the youngest, looked up to the brothers, who eventually led him into a life of horse thieving and bank and train robberies. It all came to an end in 1892 in Coffeyville, Kansas, when the gang attempted to rob two banks at the same time, thus outdoing Jessie James's gang. Unfortunately for the Dalton Gang, the townspeople got wind of the plan, armed themselves, and gathered outside, waiting for the robbers to emerge from the bank.

A gunfight broke out, and townspeople killed four of the five gang members. Emmett received twenty-three gunshot wounds and amazingly survived. He was captured, tried, and sentenced to life in prison. After fourteen years, he was released a changed man. He married his childhood sweetheart, Julia, and lived a respectable life as a tailor and then a real estate agent, author, and film consultant. Not long after he was baptized at the Angelus Temple, where I once sang, Emmett finally succumbed to a host of health problems in 1937.

Emmett Dalton

It is said that there wasn't a person alive who didn't like the reformed Emmett Dalton, and that included my parents. My brother was named Thomas Dalton Clark in honor of the neighbor they knew as a good and kind man.

Another brush with the lawless happened when I was an adult. My friends Thelma, Bennie, Norma, and I decided to live on the wild side a bit and take a trip to Las Vegas to see the shows and try our hand at gambling. I had been to Vegas many times with my parents. We—my mother in particular—liked to play the slot machines, and even though we were religiously conservative, my parents saw no harm in this form of recreation.

We wanted to make the most of our trip, so we began to ask friends where we should stay and what shows we should see. A dentist friend of a friend, who also happened to own a Gardena, California, poker club and had connections in Vegas, said, "You have to stay at the Stardust. It is the best casino and hotel in town. Once you get there, look up my friend, Hy Goldbaum. Tell him you are friends of Russ and Mary. I'll call him and let him know you are coming."

This was going to be an exciting adventure, and we could feel it in our bones.

But there were a few details to work out. "How are we going to get there?" I asked.

Thelma said, "Oh don't worry, darling. We will take the extra car." We fell into fits of laughter. The "extra car" was our secret code for the Greyhound bus.

My friends and I packed our suitcases and, in a flurry of excitement, boarded the bus in Los Angeles. Destination: Sin City, Las Vegas, Nevada! When we arrived at the bus station in Las Vegas, we claimed our luggage and took a cab to the Stardust Hotel.

We had been on the road for over six hours, so the spectacular Stardust Hotel sign was a welcome sight. With 2 percent vision, I could see only a bright light in the night sky, so my friends described the circle of stars with the name of the hotel in the center. It lit up the night with seven thousand feet of neon tubing and eleven thousand bulbs, and it was the unofficial symbol of Las Vegas at that time. How exciting it was to walk under the lights and through the doors of the main entrance of the world-famous Stardust Hotel!

Stardust Hotel

As we checked in at the reservation desk, I asked to speak to Mr. Hy Goldbaum. The man behind the desk chuckled and said, "I am sorry, miss. I can't just put you through to Mr. Goldbaum. Is there something I can help you with?"

"Just tell Mr. Goldbaum that Betty Clark and her friends are here. He knows I am coming." The man thought for a moment and then turned his back to me and mumbled into the telephone. Then he turned around and handed me the phone.

I said, "Hello?"

A powerful voice half yelled, "Who is this?"

"It is Betty Clark. I am a friend of—"

"Stay right there," he said.

I turned to my friends, wide-eyed, and whispered, "He is on his way."

I hardly got those words out before a short, barrel-chested man with dark hair and eyes came marching right by us and over to the receptionist and ordered, "Give them a room." Then he turned to us. "Who is Betty?"

"I am," I said, half raising my hand.

"OK. You all be back down here at seven o'clock sharp." And he marched off again, disappearing into the maze of one-armed bandits and craps tables.

The receptionist handed us our key and said, "Welcome to the Stardust," and we went off to the elevators and up to find our room. The beautifully decorated suite was fantastic, but we had to enjoy it later. We had only a few minutes to change and get downstairs by seven, so we raced around getting dressed.

The style of clothing for an evening in the casinos in the 1950s was formal eveningwear. Women wore elegant, floor-length gowns with glittering jewelry, and men were attired in tuxedos or, at the very least, a well-cut black suit. No one would even think of wearing anything less, and seeing the shorts and T-shirts styles of today would have made us faint dead away.

The four of us left our room in a cloud of French perfume, coiffed hair, and tastefully applied makeup, with lovely gowns swirling around our ankles. We floated through the hall to the elevator and rode down to the lobby. When the doors to the elevator parted, there was Mr. Goldbaum. He barked, "Come with me."

We followed him through the casino to the dinner theater entrance. He marched alongside the line of people waiting to get in to see the show, up to the roped entrance, unhooked the velvet rope, and motioned us past him. He hooked the rope behind him and opened the theater doors. There was a huge stage, and cloth-covered tables and chairs that filled the remainder of the room.

Mr. Goldbaum turned to me and said, "See that table over there?"

"No, I don't," I replied.

Somewhat embarrassed, he said, "Umm, yeah. Right. OK." He turned to Thelma and said, "See that table over there? That is your table. Enjoy the show."

And we did. We were waited on hand and foot. Our champagne glasses were kept full, and the delicious dinner was served with one dish after another swished in front of us. The showgirls on stage were beautiful and the music fantastic. When the lights came up and the crowd began to leave, we remained seated, waiting for our check. It did not come, so we signaled a waiter and asked for the check.

He said, "Oh, miss, there is no check. Mr. Goldbaum has taken care of it."

We left the theater in total dismay and began to make our way back to the elevators, and there was Mr. Goldbaum waiting for us. We thanked him profusely for the wonderful show and the dinner. He turned on his heel, as if he had not heard a word we said, and commanded, "Come with me."

So once again we followed Mr. Goldbaum like a row of ducks, this time to a cocktail lounge. "Drinks on me," he said as he nodded to the hostess before walking out the door, leaving us dumbfounded.

"Right this way," the hostess said. She guided us through the lounge and to a group of wonderful, soft leather chairs that were facing the live jazz band with singer Keely Smith and her sidekick husband, Louis Prima, performing. An hour and a couple of drinks later, we made our way back to our room. We flopped on the beds and began to worry.

"How much are we going to have to pay for all this?" Thelma asked, glancing around the room. "We better check with the front desk tomorrow and see what our bill is so far."

The first thing the next morning, Thelma went to the front desk to check on our bill. Thelma burst back into our room minutes later and squealed in delight, "You are not going to believe this! It is free. It is all free. Mr. Goldbaum has taken care of everything."

"You are kidding!" I said.

"No I am not," Thelma sang.

And so it was. We went downstairs, and Mr. Goldbaum would appear and escort us to another event, meal, or cocktail and then disappear. He had connections with the Flamingo and Frontier Casinos and told their managers to look after us just as he did at the Stardust. It seemed everywhere we went, he made sure we were treated royally. We, of course, were amazed at our good fortune and enjoyed ourselves tremendously.

Finally, we found time to do some gambling at the Stardust, and I settled myself in front of a slot machine with a cup full of coins. I put in a coin and hoped to hear the "ding, ding, ding" to tell me I had won. I was relaxed and having a great time when suddenly Mr. Goldbaum's voice roared behind me, nearly knocking me off my chair.

"What are you doing?"

"Geesh, you nearly scared me to death, Mr. Goldbaum. I am playing the slots."

"No, you are not. You are just going to lose your money. How do you think we make money around here?"

"Well, I came here to play the slots," I replied. "So I might as well finish what I started."

Mr. Goldbaum stomped off, and I continued dropping in one coin after another, hoping for that big hit. Then, without warning, another cup filled with silver dollars came crashing on the counter in front of me. "If you are going to play, then play with our money. And my name is Hy. Don't call me Mr. Goldbaum. It's Hy."

Before I could say anything, he was gone again, but this was the beginning of a long friendship between Hy Goldbaum and Betty Clark. He later told me he liked my spunk, and I was fascinated by his abrupt manner, which so cleverly shielded an enormous heart.

I returned to the Stardust many times during the next few years, and Hy always took care of me. One time he asked, "Is there anything you would like to do while you are here, Betty?"

"Oh, I would love to see the Rat Pack show." This was a very popular show with Frank Sinatra, Joey Bishop, Peter Lawford, Dean Martin, and Sammy Davis Jr., and it was always difficult to get tickets.

"You are not going to that show. They are a bunch of hoodlums." That was that.

There were many times when Hy and I sat down together and caught up on our personal lives. I found him to be a warm and generous man. We were not romantically involved; in fact, I visited his home several times and knew his wife, Gail.

I had heard rumors that Hy was connected to the Mafia in some way, but the subject never came up. Quite honestly, that same intrigue I felt as a girl flared up again when I was with him. The inferred danger, the mysterious code of ethics, the dark-suited men who lurked about, and the romance of it all reminded me of the stories I had heard in 1920s and '30s. The odd thing, and perhaps the most appealing aspect of being so close to the organization, was that I always felt safe and looked after when I was at the Stardust. I knew nothing bad would ever happen to me while I was in Las Vegas and under the watchful eye of Hy. And nothing ever did.

Not until recently did I learn that Hyman Goldbaum's official title was credit manager of the Stardust Hotel. He was a career criminal with fourteen convictions, had served three years in prison for income tax evasion, and had seven known aliases. The Stardust was part of the Chicago Outfit's business holdings, and it made a fortune for them. It was eventually sold to a reputable business group and went through a series of unsuccessful changes. Vegas continued to grow. Larger and more spectacular hotels and casinos surpassed the Stardust, and finally in 2007 the hotel had its last moment of international media attention when it was demolished by a series of controlled implosions. The Stardust went out in grand style, with fireworks and music.

9

ISLAND HOPPING

When a marriage ends, so does part of your identity. You are no longer Mrs. So and So. You become the "divorcee," and in the early sixties it was not the nicest title to have. When someone said, "Oh, she is a divorcee," it was synonymous with a woman who had less-than-ideal morals, "so keep a watchful eye on your husband around her." And even though I knew ending my marriage to Al was the best thing for both of us, I had a sense of loss not only of a husband but also of part of myself. I was confused about how to get myself back and what to do next.

While the divorce proceedings were underway, I got a call from my friend Aggie Green. I first met Aggie when we shared a hospital room. I had just had another eye surgery, and when I woke up, my father was there. He threw back the curtain that separated Aggie and me, pointed in my direction and declared, "This old bag is not going to make it!" The three of us all broke up in laughter, and that was the beginning of a wonderful friendship with Aggie.

"Betty," Aggie said excitedly. "Pack your bags; we are going to Hawaii!"

"What on earth are you talking about?" I asked.

Aggie explained, "Universal Studios is arranging a trip to Hawaii, complete with tours around the islands, for some of their employees. Ralph and I are going, and we want you and Virginia to go with us."

"Are you crazy, Aggie? I can't go. I am in the middle of a divorce. Besides that, I just don't feel like going."

"You better go, Betty, because I already bought your tickets, and if you don't go, I will lose my money."

Ralph and Aggie owned a large catering business that worked specifically with film studios. They went on location around the world with films that were in production, making sure that the crew and talent were well fed and pampered. They worked with Universal most often, and in gratitude Universal had offered them spots on the Hawaiian trip. Aggie, wisely knowing what I needed, scooped up four tickets. Ralph, Aggie, Virginia, and I were going to the islands!

All twenty people going on the island tour met at the Los Angeles airport and were escorted onto the plane and seated together in the same section. Virginia and I sat in a row of two seats, she by the window and I with the aisle seat. After takeoff and a couple of hours into the trip, I excused myself to Virginia and headed toward bathrooms at the back of the plane. I balanced myself as I walked through the vibrating plane by holding on to the backs of the aisle seats. Suddenly a hand reached up and grabbed my arm, startling me.

A man said, "Where are you going?" Was he stupid? Where else would I be going but to the bathroom?

"None of your business," I mumbled. He chuckled, and when I returned to my seat, I made sure I was walking on the opposite side of the aisle from his seat. I learned his name was Ted and he was with our tour group. It was not the last time I ran into this character.

We arrived in Honolulu tired but excited. Virginia and I checked into our room at the Halekulani Hotel, unpacked, and decided to go out for a drink. We found our way to the Surfrider Beach Bar, which was highly recommended, and sank into our seats with that sigh people exhale when they have found paradise. But no sooner had we sat down when a couple of men from the bar yelled out, "Where are you girls from?"

"LA," we responded.

"No kidding? So are we. May we join you?"

They sat down at our table and introduced themselves. "I am Sam Yorty, and this is my friend Karl Rundberg."

"Have you seen Pearl Harbor yet? We will take you on a private tour. Meet us at the information center at nine tomorrow morning."

"Sure," we said, not believing a word they said. After some polite conversation Virginia and I headed off to our rooms for a good night's sleep before we began our three-week tour of the islands.

As it turned out, Virginia and I did have a tour of Pearl Harbor on our schedule at ten, so we got up, showered, had breakfast, and caught our ride to Pearl Harbor. We arrived a bit early, so we walked around the area until the tour started.

All of a sudden we heard, "Where the hell have you been? We have been calling you over the PA for the last twenty minutes." We did have a private guide at Pearl Harbor who told us of the horrors of that day. I could clearly recall that lazy day on the beach in Santa Monica when I first heard of the bombings and how that memory was etched in my mind forever.

We waved good-bye to Sam and Karl and continued on our scheduled activities with the Universal Studios group. As it turned out, Sam Yorty became the mayor of Los Angeles, and Karl Rundberg was a city councilman during the same time. The two men were often at odds with each other, but both had fascinating and controversial careers we followed for years.

Throughout the Hawaiian tour, I caught glimpses of the man who had grabbed my arm on the plane. He was always helping someone off the bus or carrying someone's bags, and he always seemed to be trying to get my attention. I was aloof. He was friendly. Too friendly maybe.

Virginia and I were having a wonderful time and often met up with Aggie and Ralph. Our rooms were luxurious, and we were treated like royalty everywhere we went. When we arrived in Maui, we once again went directly to our hotel room to unpack and found it to be the most spectacular accommodations of any we'd had on the trip. We thought we might want to stay there forever. As we were putting our things away, we heard a knock at the door. I walked across the room to the door and asked, "Who is it?"

"It's me, Ted. May I speak with you a minute?"

I hesitated and then opened the door. "Come in. What can I do for you?"

"Will you go to dinner with me?"

Before I could even give Ted an answer, Virginia, said, "Go, go, I'll be fine." And then she nearly shoved me out the door.

Ted and I found a little café on the beach with live music. We talked as we ate dinner, and I learned that Ted was sound supervisor on many films and television shows. He liked pets, cats in particular, and sparkling burgundy, which was what we were drinking at the time. I learned he was going through a divorce too. I felt very comfortable with him, and it surprised me.

After dinner, we went down to the ocean's edge, took off our shoes, wiggled our toes in the warm sand, and walked until we could no longer hear the music from the café. The night was warm, with just a hint of a breeze coming from the ocean. Ted spread a blanket on the sand, and we sat and talked again, this time almost whispering.

Maybe it was sparkling burgundy or the hypnotic sound of the water lapping against the shore that caused Ted and me to lose the sensible inhibitions we might have had on any other night. Suddenly we were kissing passionately and then making sweet, gentle love to the rhythm of the ocean waves. We talked for a while longer, sharing stories of events in our lives, and then headed back to my hotel. Ted walked me to me to my door, kissed me again, and said good-night. I could not believe I had been totally swept off my feet in less than five hours.

I spent time with Ted every day until the end of our trip. Oddly, he had become quite proper and gentleman-ly, especially if there was anyone else around. There was no repeat of the interlude on the beach. I was confused, but he was attentive and sweet, and I continued to enjoy his company. In the back of my mind, however, I kept wondering if this had been just a one-night stand and if, after the trip, he would go back to his life without a thought of me.

The dream vacation was coming to a close, and I was so grateful to Aggie for insisting that I go. I felt better prepared to face the finality of my divorce from Al and felt I had regained some of my self-confidence.

We all boarded the plane with the "Hawaiian Wedding Song" playing over the plane's PA system, and that's when it hit me: the vacation was over. I began to get teary-eyed. Virginia glanced over at me from her window seat. "Betty, what's wrong?" she said, clearly alarmed.

"I don't want to leave."

"Oh, for God's sake, Betty. You can always come back."

"But," I sputtered, "I will never see Ted again."

"Betty, fasten your safety belt and think of the good times."

The plane took off, and I was still sniffling and struggling to hold back a real sobbing session. Virginia said, "Excuse me," and stepped over me into the aisle. "I am going back to sit with John." As soon as she was in the aisle, Ted slid right into the now-empty seat next to me.

"So what's all this fuss about?"

Without an ounce of pride left in me, I blurted out, "I'll never see you again, and I—"

"Betty," Ted said. "You think this is the end? No, honey, it is the beginning." And it was.

10

A WHOLE NEW WORLD

Our group returned from the Universal Studios sponsored Hawaiian tour late in the evening. I finally rounded up my luggage, caught a cab, and arrived home at about ten o'clock. I opened the front door and walked into that wonderful feeling of home one experiences after a long trip. I dropped my suitcases in the hallway and began to unpack but changed my mind and decided to head straight for the comfort of my own bed instead. Despite being exhausted, I could not fall asleep, so I tossed and turned through the night, trying to get comfortable enough to relax.

Memories of the trip whirled around in my head, and I couldn't help wondering if the time with Ted was just a vacation romance. Had I made a fool of myself? We had exchanged addresses and phone numbers. I held the card from him that I had taken to bed with me. And though I could not see the words printed on the card, I knew it read "Edwin Ted Hodgett," with his telephone number printed neatly below. Had he tossed my phone number into a file with hundreds of other women's phone numbers? Would I really ever see him again as he promised? "It will all be OK. It will all be OK," I told myself, and I finally drifted off just as the sun was coming up.

At seven, my phone rang, waking me from unsatisfying sleep. It was Ted.

"What are you doing?" he asked enthusiastically.

"Are you kidding me!" I shot back groggily. "I am trying to sleep."

"Well, get up. I'm coming over," he said just before he hung up.

I shot out of bed and scrambled around the house, got dressed, and picked up clothing that was scattered about from my unpacking efforts the night before.

Everything was just about in order when I heard a car come to a screeching halt in the driveway. Ted leapt out of his white Karmann Ghia convertible and waved at my stunned father, who had been fixing a lawnmower in his yard next door. Ted yelled over, "Hiya, Tom!" Then he bounded up the fifteen steps to my front door and banged on it until I answered.

"For heaven's sake, Ted. I haven't even had time to tell my dad about you yet."

He just laughed and twirled me around. "It is the beginning, Betty!"

Ted quickly introduced me to his world, and it was a totally different world from anything I had ever known. He worked in sound production for television and film and had begun his career as a sound boom man in the 1957 film *Omar Khayyam*.

Ted and Betty

Geographically, I could not have been any closer to the film industry. Los Angeles, my hometown, was and still is the undisputed center of the motion picture universe. Yet I knew absolutely nothing more about the business of film making than what I, and millions of other people, saw on the silver screen.

It was a whirlwind romance with Ted. He was fun, adventurous, and doting. He took me to the film sets where he was working. He introduced me to celebrities, and we attended more parties and events than I could count. I learned how to drink Scotch and eat caviar.

Ted was working on television shows such as *Gunsmoke, The Wonderful World of Golf, The Mary Tyler Moore Show,* and *60 Minutes,* as well as a number of films. He was traveling quite a bit, and he worried about me while he was gone.

One evening after dinner, he said, "Today I drove by a place in LA that helps people with low vision. It is called Braille Institute. Have you ever thought about volunteering there?"

I was caught off guard. "Of course I have. Why would I want to do that? I really don't have time."

"Betty, are you just going to spend the rest of your life in your parents' candy factory?" he asked. "Don't you want to broaden your experiences and do something a little different and maybe even help someone in the process? I have donated money to Braille for years, and they offer wonderful services."

"Ted, I am just fine with my life the way it is. Now let's talk about something else."

For me the subject was definitely closed. I did not want to isolate myself by being only with blind people like I had been when I was in elementary school. I had escaped that and was not going back.

About a week later, Ted came home and said, "Come on, Betty. It is a beautiful day. Let's go for a ride." I was game, so we jumped in the car and drove a few miles around Los Angeles. Then Ted drove up in front of a big building and said, "OK, let's get out."

"Ted," I said, not recognizing the building at first, "Where are we?"

"Remember we talked about Braille Institute last week?"

"Oh no you don't," I nearly shouted.

"Betty, get out of the car. We are just going in to look around."

An hour later I came out the front door of the building as a most reluctant enrolled student and registered volunteer in their Public Speakers' Bureau. As the weeks went by, I really began to enjoy my work, and it did not go unnoticed by the administration. Two months after I first walked through the doors, I was called into the director's office.

"Betty," he said, "we are very happy with the work you are doing, and we would like to move you to a new position. We would like you to become a staff member in our public relations department."

Oh my gosh! I had a job that was not in a "candy factory." I had not realized how protected and predictable my world had become. My sense of security was still literally tied to my family's apron strings, and it was time for me to grow up and become truly independent. I was grateful for all my parents had sacrificed and done for me, and they were grateful that I had the courage to take this next step toward independence.

Ted was ecstatic when I told him. "I am so proud of you, Betty!" he exclaimed. "You will have a lot of interesting opportunities that you cannot even imagine." Ted was right. I did meet wonderful people and visited so many interesting places. I became a skilled and sought after public speaker and consultant. Life was fantastic.

Through my job, I became involved with an exhibition square dancing group. All of us in the group had low vision in varying degrees and danced not only in the exhibition group but also in regular square dancing clubs. I really enjoyed square dancing and told Ted about all I had learned and even demonstrated my moves for him. I was not sure he understood all that square dancing involved, but he always seemed to enjoy my stories and news about practice and performing.

Our square dance exhibition group's big moment came when an international convention of square dancers was held in the Convention Center in Los Angeles. I designed the costumes for our group, and we practiced endlessly. Then, in front of a crowd of two thousand, we took center stage and performed flawlessly. The crowd rose to its feet and gave us a long and loud standing ovation.

My relationship with Ted was the best it had ever been, or so it seemed to me. But he had become secretive and evasive about unexplained evenings at work. I knew the symptoms of a crumbling relationship all too well, and this time I decided not to spend years ignoring the obvious. I was going to catch him in the act. I called my favorite sidekick, my aunt Virginia, and we laid out a plan.

Ted yelled, "Betty, I am going out. Love you. See you later."

The front door slammed before I could respond. Virginia just *happened* to be visiting on Ted's usual "going out" night, and as soon as that door slammed, the two of us raced down the front stairs, jumped in her car, and took off after Ted. The white Karmann Ghia was not hard to spot, and within minutes we were on his tail. We followed him for about ten miles until we saw him stop and park his car on the street.

He got out and walked about half a block and went into a building. Virginia parked, and we tore out of the car, crossed the street, and snuck along the side of the building, hugging the wall like cat burglars. We came to the door that Ted had gone through and saw sign taped to a small window next to the door: "Square Dance Lessons Tonight 7 to 9 P.M. Don't be late!" I nearly sank to the ground. My sweet Teddy was taking square dance lessons! I was so ashamed that I had I mistrusted him, and I never did tell him what Virginia and I had done.

A few months later, Ted came home exhausted from a film shoot in Arizona. "I am just so tired," he said as he sank into the sofa. "I don't know what is wrong with me. I can't seem to keep my balance. I don't know—maybe it was just the heat, but I just don't feel well at all. I am going to bed." Ted went to bed and was soon asleep, but when he woke the next morning, he was not feeling any better, so I insisted he go to the doctor.

After an exam and several tests, the news from Ted's doctor was devastating. Ted had Parkinson's disease, a degenerative disease of the central nervous system. The prognosis for Ted was grim. He was already showing signs of the disease with mild tremors.

Ted and I went to classes and programs at University of California–Los Angeles (UCLA) on how to live with Parkinson's. We tried to take in all the information we could, hoping there had been a mistake and he did not really have Parkinson's at all. But his disease progressed just as the doctors, the books, and the literature said it would.

We heard of a new brain surgery that could control the tremors, and we felt hopeful. We asked the doctor if Ted was a good candidate for the surgery and what were the best and the worst-case scenarios. The doctor laid out all the conceivable outcomes including the possibility that Ted could become a quadriplegic if the surgery did not go well. Ted and I decided that the risk was far too great and dismissed the idea entirely. We went home and followed all the directions for diet and exercise, in the hopes we could slow the inevitable deterioration of his nervous system.

We finally came to grips with the reality that things would become progressively worse, but Ted continued to do things just as he always had. Once a week, he took the lawn mower from the garage, wheeled it to the foot of the fifteen stairs that led to the grassy area behind our tri-level home. Once finished he hauled the mower back down the stairs. Each week it seemed to take a little longer to complete this task, but he never complained. And he never lost his sense of humor.

One day, while on his daily therapeutic walks, Ted stopped for a rest on a neighborhood bench. A boy about six years old came up to him and said, "Mister, you are shaking."

"Yup," Ted answered.

"Do you know you are shaking?"

"Yup," Ted said once again.

"Well, then stop it."

Ted later told me of the incident, and he could not stop laughing. But as time went on, the situation became less and less funny. Ted had trouble sleeping, walking, and feeding himself. I worried that I would not be able to continue caring for him.

"Ted," I said, "we need to talk about what we are going to do. Let's look into the services the Motion Picture and Television Country Home and Hospital have to offer. I want you to have the best care possible."

He looked at me sternly. "I have worked with those people all my life. I don't want to die with them. I get the best care right here with you." I thought about all he had done for me over the years and never brought up the subject again.

Ted and I never married but that didn't lessen our devotion to each other. His commitment to me was just as strong as mine was to him. When I had eye surgery in a hospital on the outskirts of Los Angeles, Ted, who could no longer drive, took the hour-and-a-half trip by bus to the hospital. He changed buses twice and stumbled along for three blocks before reaching the hospital. I could not believe it when he came through the door of my room. I have never been so overwhelmed by love as the moment he walked through the door and literally fell into my arms and onto my hospital bed.

On New Year's Eve, Ted and I decided to have a small celebration at home with just the two of us. I was in the kitchen fixing our meal for the evening when I heard Ted get into the shower. I went into the dining room and was setting the table when I heard a loud thump coming from the bedroom. I knew immediately that Ted had fallen. I rushed into the bedroom and found him on the floor, gasping for breath. I leaned over, "Oh God, Teddy, hang on. I am going to call for help." I ran to the phone and dialed 911. I gave the operator our name and address and explained the situation. She assured me help was on the way.

I rushed back to Ted, only to find his breathing was much worse. I sat on the floor and moved his head at an angle onto my lap, hoping that would keep him from choking. I waited and waited for the ambulance to arrive, and after several minutes, I rested Ted's head on a towel and ran out of the bedroom to the front door. I opened it to listen for the sound of sirens. Nothing. I went out the front door, down the stairs, and to the end of the driveway, frantically looking to see if the ambulance was coming. The station was only three blocks away. Where were they? I ran back into the house and called 911 again.

"Where are you? Ted is going to die if you don't get here soon."

"Ma'am, you gave us the wrong address."

"Oh my God! I did not! Here is my address again. Please, please hurry." I then called my mother, who lived next door, and asked her to go outside and watch for the ambulance.

By this time I was sobbing. I returned to the bedroom and got back on the floor with Ted. "Please, Teddy, please. Hold on, help is coming."

The EMT personnel burst through the door, moved Ted onto a gurney, and took us by ambulance to the Hollywood Presbyterian Hospital. Ted died there an hour later.

I was encased in a grief so strong I thought I would never, ever escape. Comfort came in one night when I awoke to find Ted at the end of the bed. "Come here," he called to me. I went to him and sat on his lap. "I want you to stop crying. I am all right now. You see? No tremors. No pain. You wouldn't want me to come back and experience that again, would you?" Tears flung across my face as I shook my head no. "Now go back to bed and be happy. I'll always love you." I went back to bed feeling content and slept peacefully.

The next morning I woke up and immediately recalled Ted's visit. It all seemed too real to have been a dream. The bedroom door was closed and locked as it always was. How did Ted get in?

I cannot explain this event, but I have heard that my experience was not uncommon. Is it our minds that take over to comfort us or is it a real visit from the other side to help us through our grief? The event had such an unnerving impact on me that I still ponder it today.

11

*F*OUND

*T*he phone rang as I was just about ready to go out the door. I hesitated. *Should I answer it or hope the caller rings back?* I thought. *Oh, darn.* I threw my purse on the sofa and scurried over to the phone.

"Hello."

"Is this Betty Clark?" a familiar male voice asked.

I drew in a long, deep breath. "Stuart Mong. I would recognize your voice anywhere! Do you know I have adored you for forty-two years?"

He laughed. "How are you, Betty?" And that is how the best part of my life began.

Stu explained that he had just opened a box that had been in storage and found my telephone number in a letter his sister had sent a year before. "She apparently thought I received the letter, and since I didn't mention receiving your phone number, she thought neither should she."

Stu and I talked in detail about the events during the past forty-two years of our lives. There was so much to catch up on. I learned about his life in the service, his schooling, and his career in museum administration. I told him about Al and Ted and my work at Braille Institute. He talked of his failed marriage. Hours later we finally hung up, and I still could not believe I had heard from him after all that time.

Soon we were talking daily, and it was getting expensive. Long-distance calls were charged by the minute back then, and the bills began to add up fast. I did not want to send letters, because I would need someone to read Stu's letters to me and that did not allow for any privacy. So we decided to send audiotapes back and forth. One day a box arrived from Stu that was larger than the usual tape packages. I opened it, and there was a wooden, hand-carved, heart-shaped block with a small hurdy-gurdy music machine, as you would find in a music box, secured on top. I turned the crank to hear the music play. It was "As Time Goes By." I was so touched that he still remembered the song that had played during our first dance at the Palladium in 1942! I was beginning to feel like a lovesick teenager; I could not help playing the music box and the tapes from Stu over and over again.

Four months went by, and it was evident that the little spark we had in 1943 had now flared up into a very warm and lovely flame.

Stu called and announced, "I have decided to take a road trip to visit an old friend in Oklahoma and would like to continue driving west and end up in California to see you."

"Oh Stu, that would be wonderful." I nearly giggled with glee. We continued talking about his trip, and then I suggested, "What if I fly to Oklahoma City and we drive to LA together?"

"Would you really do that?" Stu asked, surprised by my suggestion. "That would be great if you are sure you really want to."

"I do want to," I said, and I began to make plans in my head. When my friends got wind of my plans, they called. They came over. They met me at work. "You are crazier than hell. Have you lost your mind? You haven't seen this guy in a hundred years. He could be a serial killer by now." I went anyway.

In the early spring of 1984, I boarded a flight from Los Angeles to Denver. I was wearing a lovely pink ultra-suede suit with matching heels and handbag. In Denver I would get a connecting flight to Oklahoma City, and Stu would meet me at the airport at nine o'clock.

The flight to Denver was uneventful until we were about twenty minutes away from the airport. The stewardess came on the intercom. "Ladies and gentlemen, it seems we are heading into a bit of a snowstorm. Please stay in your seats, and keep your seatbelts fastened until we land."

A snowstorm? Oops! I had no overcoat, boots, or gloves. I was from Southern California. Who thinks about snowstorms? Then came, "Ladies and gentlemen, we are unable to land until the runway is cleared, so if it seems we are flying around in circles, we are. Those of you who had a connecting flight to Oklahoma, that flight departed early. Please check in at the gate so we can arrange for another flight for you." My heart sank as I wondered if poor Stu was waiting and worried.

An hour later we were able to land, and we were all herded into the airport, where we were told that all flights had been delayed. Meanwhile, Stu had arrived at the airport in Oklahoma City, only to learn my flight was going to be late. This was, of course, before cell phones were available, so Stu had no other information other than the flight would be delayed for goodness knows how long.

Stu and I sat in our airports, miles and miles apart, hour after hour, until finally I boarded a connecting flight for Oklahoma City. We landed at two o'clock in the morning. I was cold, tired, and hungry, and my pink suit was crumpled beyond repair. It was not the way a lady would like to have the man of her dreams see her for the first time in forty-three years. The stewardess escorted me off the plane, and Stu was waiting at the gate. He came up and told the stewardess, "Thank you. I'll take over from now on."

Stu and I hugged, not quite believing this was really happening, but both of us were way too tired to question anything. We got into the car and drove to a hotel, where Stu had reserved a room. On the way I mentioned I had not eaten and was starving. By then it was nearly three in the morning and nothing was open. Stu reached into his pocket and pulled out a packet of Red Hots, and that was our first meal together.

When we got to our hotel room, all I wanted to do was take a hot shower to get warm. I went into the bathroom, closed the door, let my clothes fall to the floor, and stepped into the shower. No shower before or since has ever felt as good. I turned the water as hot as I could stand it to warm my weary bones. Then I heard a *tap, tap, tap* on the shower door. "May I come in?" I heard Stu say.

I replied, "I was hoping you would."

The next day, we happily piled into Stu's Camry and headed for California. We decided we had time to take three days for the drive to Los Angeles. It would be an unhurried drive, and I would still have time to be back at work by Monday.

On the first day of the drive, Stu began talking, and it was as if his personal dam had broken. He could not seem to get the words and emotions out fast enough. There were years and years worth of stories of his successes and of his disappointments. His marriage had been in trouble since the beginning, and he honorably had stuck it out. But he finally could no longer bear life with a coldhearted woman he did not love. My phone number had appeared at the perfect time, he said. And the four months we had taken to get to know each other by long distance had made him think he might have one last chance at happiness. I felt the same, and just being in the car with him for three days was more than I could have imagined six months earlier.

As we approached Los Angeles, I began to give Stu detailed street and landmark directions to my house. He turned to me and said, "How do you do that!"

"Do what?" I said, knowing exactly what he was talking about.

"How do you know all the names of the streets and where they are if you can't see them?"

"Stu, I have lived here all my life. I know every inch of LA like the back of my hand." And it was true. I did know LA, and Stu never needed a map or a GPS as long as he had me in the car with him.

We pulled up into my driveway and unloaded the suitcases from the car into the hallway of my house. Then we walked down the street to my mother's house so I could properly introduce him. I thought it was sweet that he seemed a little nervous to meet her, but she liked him immediately.

On Monday I had a speaking engagement at Lake Arrowhead, California, and I threw poor Stu right into the middle of my world. He drove us there, and I spoke to a Rotary group. Afterward I introduced him to my friend Thelma and her husband. Other friends joined us. The guys kidnapped Stu and took him on a tour of the area while the rest of us made plans for dinner. Stu enjoyed himself tremendously.

It soon was evident that Stu was never going back to the Midwest, and I could not have been happier. It is usually a little awkward moving into someone else's house, so I did all I could to make him feel it was his home too. I turned the spare bathroom into a walk-in closet for him, and we created his own private workspace by putting a desk in the bedroom for his computer.

At first I worried Stu might become bored in California. He had arthritis in his hands, so he could no longer paint or play the violin. Soon he was volunteering at Braille, reading, and doing odd jobs around the house and could not have been happier. I no longer needed a car and driver, because he delighted in taking me to my speaking engagements, whether they were across town or hundreds of miles away. We entertained and dined out with friends often. Stu gave himself a makeover by having his hair styled and bought a new California wardrobe. His Midwestern friends could not believe the new Stu.

Stu and I had to attend the funeral of the wife of an ophthalmologist friend of mine. He and his wife had lived a long and happy life together, and he was so distraught at the funeral that we could not help feel the pain he was experiencing. This particularly touched Stu. During the service, he took my hand and sniffed, "I think we should get married." It was quite an emotional day. Not every girl gets a proposal at a funeral.

In November of 1988, Stu and I invited twelve friends for a Palm Springs weekend at the Ritz Carlton Resort. We were married there in a lovely ceremony with a harpist, candlelight, and a champagne dinner following. It was perfect.

Betty and Stu's Wedding

One of our favorite places was the Bob Burns Supper Club off Wilshire Boulevard in Santa Monica. Since I spoke in that area often, it was a nice place to pop in and have a drink and a sandwich. On our first visit, we realized it was a piano bar and the man at the piano had a wonderful voice. After we heard a couple of songs, Stu suggested we go talk to the musician.

We walked over to the piano, and Stu said, "We are really enjoying your music. My name is Stu, and this is my wife, Betty."

"Nice to meet you, Stu. My name is Howlett Smith." They shook hands. "And nice to meet you, Betty." Then there was an awkward silence. He said, "Betty, I am blind. If you would like to shake hands, you will have to put your hand in mine."

I burst out laughing. "I was about to say the same thing to you!"

Howlett instantly became our friend. Unbeknownst to us at the time, he had quite an impressive background. He had graduated as a music major from the University of Arizona and was a member of the El Camino College faculty, teaching in the applied music program. He is a prolific songwriter, vocal and piano coach, whistler, and choir director. He has been involved in radio, TV, and films and was the music director of the Broadway show, *Me and Bessie*, as well as having a recurring role on *General Hospital*. His songs "Let's Go Where the Grass Is Greener," "Little Altar Boy," and "It's the Last Day of Summer" were some of our favorites. Howlett was listed in *Los Angeles* magazine as one of the three hundred reasons to stay in Los Angeles, and he was the reason we kept going back to the Bob Burns Supper Club.

Howlett Smith Photo Credit: Randall Richards

We told him our story of meeting again after so many years. He said, "OK, I am playing this song just for you two. It is my own composition." Then he sang, "You Never Let Me Down." We went back several times just to hear him and always requested he play and sing his song and, of course, "As Time Goes By." Life was very, very good.

Stu and I lived very comfortably in Los Angeles, but the traffic was getting worse every year. Stu had never had an accident, yet I could tell all the driving had become nerve-racking for him. Even so, he would not hear of anyone else driving me. I worried the situation was taking a toll on his health and well-being. I thought the best solution would be to ask for a transfer to the Braille Institute Center in Rancho Mirage near Palm Springs, California. The pace there was a little slower, and there was not nearly the traffic there was in Los Angeles.

The transfer came through, and Stu and I sold our house in Los Angeles and moved into a beautiful home in Palm Desert. It made sense at the time.

12

$\mathcal{T}$ R I U M P H

$\mathcal{D}$oheny Eye Institute in Los Angeles is one of the top ten ophthalmology centers in the United States. It also ranks in the top ten programs in National Institute of Health funding for vision research.

Carrie Estelle Doheny, the wife of a wealthy California oilman, founded the institute in 1947 after she lost her vision from glaucoma. She realized the importance of ophthalmic care and vision research and began her organization in two rooms of St. Vincent Hospital in downtown Los Angeles. Over the years, the now-independent, nonprofit institute has grown to become a world leader in vision research, advanced patient care, and education. The University of Southern California ophthalmology faculty, part of the Keck School of Medicine of USC, provides patient care services in the Doheny Eye Institute building. I was often asked to speak to Doheny's faculty, staff, and new residents-in-training about my experiences living with limited vision. On one occasion, one of the doctors came up, congratulated me on my speech, and said, "Betty, we think you would be a good candidate for a cornea transplant. If it is something you would be interested in, please come and see me."

I was stunned. I had never even dared to hope for such an opportunity. "I will think about it," I answered. I did know about cornea transplants and that I had to consider the risks just as much as the benefits. What if my eyes rejected the grafts? What if infection set in? What if the surgery didn't work and I lost what little vision I had? But what if I could see? Really see!

I went over all these questions, fears, and possibilities with my husband. Finally, I told him, "Stu, I am going to do it. I am going to have the transplant surgery." My ever-supportive husband responded, "And I will be right there with you."

A cornea transplant, also known as corneal grafting, is when corneal tissue is donated from a recently deceased person to replace the diseased or damaged corneal tissue of an otherwise healthy patient. Very simply put, the donated cornea is cut to the same size as the tissue that is being removed. It is then sutured into place in the patient's eye, thus restoring varying degrees of vision.

The pre-surgery appointments for examination and tests were made to make sure my eyes were healthy enough for the procedure. We waited for my doctor, Dr. Ronald Smith, professor and chairman of the department of ophthalmology at Keck School of Medicine and the Doheny Eye Institute, to review all the results. He is one of the three founding clinicians of the Institute and someone in whom I could easily place my trust.

We met him in his office a few days later, and he gave us the good news: I could have the surgery done. He cautioned us that the results vary from patient to patient. In some cases, new illnesses or injuries could cause the grafts to fail, even years after the surgery. He also explained that about 20 percent of the twenty-eight thousand corneal transplants done each year failed due to rejection. My case was even more of a problem because of the underlying inflammation due to the effects of juvenile arthritis. Undaunted, I elected to proceed.

I was so fortunate to live close to one of the world's largest eye banks, the Lions Doheny Eye Bank. It was not so much a bank as it was a processing point. At that time, the demand was usually higher than the supply, so surgical-grade corneas were scarce. We waited until donor tissue became available. Once the doctors agreed it was a good match, the procedure was performed.

The surgery went off without a hitch, and a couple of days later the bandages came off and I was sent home with glasses and greatly improved vision. I was a seeing person!

I was so deeply grateful that the talent, skills, and kindness of Dr. Smith had resulted in such an amazing gift. My vision improved daily, and I could see details like the white lines down the centers of roads. I could see all the brightly colored, shiny cars. I could see flowers and trees. It was so overwhelming at times that I had trouble taking it all in. Stu and I rejoiced and planned trips to see all the things I had dreamed about and all the things he had hoped to show me one day.

I had always wanted to see Washington, D.C. The Capitol, the White House, the Lincoln Memorial, and the Smithsonian were all on our list. Stu had been a museum curator for many years, and the Smithsonian, even though on a much larger scale, was an environment where he was very comfortable. He was my own personal guide as we visited the many exhibits.

Stu and Betty

The Smithsonian's National Portrait Gallery is an art gallery of portraits of Americans who contributed to the development of our country. There are portraits of presidents, artists, performers, inventors, writers, politicians, and others who define American culture. Stu and I explored the exhibitions and collections and came to a large painting of a woman in a blue dress. I studied the portrait for several minutes, and tears inexplicably rolled down my cheeks. I turned to Stu and sobbed, "Why am I so emotional about this painting?"

Stu hugged me and said, "I believe it is because it is the first time you have seen all the details of such a lovely face in a portrait. The artist painted her expression in such a way that it has touched your heart."

This was such a new experience for me—to see an image with my two eyes and then have that image travel to my brain for interpretation, to my heart for comprehension, and then back to my eyes to produce a flood of tears, all within a matter of seconds. Having so much sight was still very new to me, and I finally truly understood that what one sees with eyes can evoke very strong reactions and emotions.

Stu and I were about to leave the Smithsonian when Stu saw a large crowd of people marching by the building. "We are never going to get out of here," he said to me. Then he asked a guard what was going on.

"It is a demonstration that has something to do with a big quilt and people who have AIDS," he replied, directing us to a side exit.

"Let's go this way," Stu said, leading me away from the crowd.

"No, come on," I said, pulling him in the other direction toward the action. "Let's go see what is going on. I have never seen a demonstration." We went down the stairs, merged with the crowd, and began to ask the people walking beside us where they were going and what this was all about. It was the NAMES Project Memorial Quilt, they explained. The quilt was on display on the National Mall.

The quilt was enormous. It was made of three-by-six-foot panels (the size of a grave). Each panel had the names of men, women, and children who had died of AIDS embroidered on multicolored fabric. The panels had been assembled into twelve-by-twelve-foot sections to make one quilt, and hundreds of quilts made up the NAMES Quilt. Discrimination and fear had resulted in many AIDS victims being abandoned by their families, shunned by their communities, denied treatment at hospitals, and refused burial by mortuaries. The NAMES Quilt was the only real recognition of their lives, their struggles, and their passing.

People were marching in support of the project and to bring attention to the terrible AIDS pandemic and the urgent need for more medical care and research to save lives. The triumphant joy of accomplishment among the marchers was contagious, and Stu and I couldn't help but join in. We chatted with folks as we walked along and collected a stack of business cards. The marchers seemed to be from every walk of life; it was interesting to see the diversity in hometowns, race, education, and employment.

Stu and I became part of history on October 11, 1987, when we, by chance, joined the national march on Washington for lesbian and gay rights. It was an experience that enriched our understanding and compassion regarding the social stigma attached to people with AIDS and the issue of equal rights for the gay and lesbian population in our country.

13

TRAGEDY

As we all know, life has its ups and downs. No one, it seems, could swing higher or sink lower than I did at times. The loss of my parents, other family members, and friends were all very sad occasions that affected me deeply. The medical challenges and surgeries I underwent were often roller-coaster rides, both physically and emotionally. But I seemed to have amazing "bounce-ability." I could bounce back from just about anything.

We returned from our Washington, D.C. adventure to Los Angeles, and I went back to work at Braille Institute. I spoke to many service clubs about the services offered by Braille Institute and my experiences living with limited vision. On my calendar was a talk at a local Lions Club. I had spoken to several Lions Clubs previously and applauded their commitment to their work to restore sight around the world, so I really looked forward to that engagement.

Stu drove me to the restaurant in Los Angeles where the Lions were holding their meeting and sat at the back of the room and listened while I spoke. The Lions members were attentive, and when my speech was over, they surrounded me with questions and comments. Once the crowd broke up and began to leave the restaurant, I found Stu and said, "Finally! Before we head home, I need to stop at the restroom."

We followed the waiter's directions to the restroom and went to the back of the restaurant and down a hallway to the door marked "Ladies." Stu said, "I'll wait for you here," and posted himself outside the door.

I pushed open the door and walked into a darkened bathroom. There were no lights on, and it was nearly pitch-black in the room. I fumbled around the wall to find the light switch, and suddenly my feet came out from under me and I was tumbling down a flight of stairs. My head bounced on each of the ten cement stairs, and I landed hard at the foot of the staircase. I lay there, the contents of my purse scattered around me, breathless and struggling to stay conscious. I was in shock—so much so that I did not think to call out for help.

After a few minutes, Stu opened the door and called out, "Betty, are you all right?"

Hearing his voice brought me around and into a full panic. "Stu, watch out for the stairs! I am down here."

Stu stood on a small landing at the top of the stairs, not believing the strange layout of the bathroom. To get to the sinks and stalls, one had to go down a flight of cement stairs. In the dark, the stairway was barely visible. Stu flicked on the light and rushed down the stairs and to my side. "Are you OK, Betty?"

"Yes, I am fine. Just help me up."

"I am not so sure," Stu said. "We better get you to a hospital and have you checked over."

At the hospital emergency room, it was discovered that I had fractured my wrist and had a big goose egg on my head. My wrist was put in a cast, and I was told to go home and get some rest.

After a few days of recovery, Stu and I decided to go to a musical concert at the Hollywood Bowl to celebrate our first outing since the fall. As we were walking to our seat, I noticed that I saw white spots everywhere and whispered to Stu, "The lighting is sure weird in here. I see spots everywhere."

"I don't see any spots. Are you sure you are OK?"

I assured him I was, but by morning the spots became a veil I could barely see through. We called Dr. Smith, and he asked us to come in immediately. The doctor peered into my eyes with various instruments and said, "There has been some damage done here, most likely from your fall. We don't know exactly how much damage there is without taking you into surgery."

The procedure was scheduled, and when I awoke after the surgery, Stu was at my side. The doctor came in a couple of hours later and said, "I am so sorry to tell you, Betty, but your retinas are detached in both eyes. The damage is such that there is nothing we can do to stop it. I do not know how much longer you will have your sight."

Both Stu and I were stunned. This was not the news I had hoped to hear. We knew this would be another situation I would have to adjust to. I suddenly realized that for most of my life I'd had the good fortune to have 2 percent vision. Now I would most likely have nothing.

I went home with some hazy vision left. Stu did everything he could think of to make the transition easier for me, including putting a light under the kitchen cabinets so I could see while cooking. We had no idea how long it would be before I would not be able to see again.

Every day my vision got a bit worse. It was as if someone were dimming the lights little by little. Then one morning I awoke, and I could see nothing. I distinctly remember everything that happened that morning. I got out of bed and made my way to the kitchen. I turned on the radio, and I could still hear. I turned on the coffee, and I could still smell. I grabbed a strawberry from the bowl on the table, and I could still taste. I washed my hands in the sink, and I could still feel. I sat down at the table with my cup of coffee, and I could still move. I was so grateful for those abilities. The only thing I had lost was my sight. I was going to be all right. Then I thought, *Yikes, what time is it? I have to get to work.*

I went into the bathroom, washed my face, brushed my teeth, put on my makeup, and brushed my hair. Then I went to my closet, chose an outfit and jewelry to wear, and got dressed. I called to Stu, who was in the living room reading the morning paper, "I am ready to go to work." And off we went. It was as simple as that.

14

THE JOYS OF WORK

There seem to be two constants woven through my life: working and being on stage with a microphone in my hand.

I have always worked. At eighteen months old, I became crippled with juvenile arthritis, and at age three, I began my first job. My parents were overwhelmed with medical bills and were barely able to put food on the table. My early talent and enthusiasm for singing turned into a lucrative career, which carried our family through those tough financial times. My father did get back on his feet, and in a big way; he had determination, he was a hard worker, and he had a good head for business. In the 1920s he found a job as a baking demonstrator to promote a brand of flour. He developed his own fruitcake recipe, which became very popular, and he sold the packaged fruitcakes on his own for extra income.

The city of San Jose, California, one of the areas where he worked, sent him an official certificate of recognition signed by the president of the council of the city stating, "The improvement of the quality of baking merchandise in the city of San Jose is now the subject of favorable comment and to your visits to San Jose as a demonstrator can be attributed [to] this marked improvement. San Jose is very appreciative of your fine work and extends a hearty welcome to visit this city whenever possible." This wonderful endorsement gave my father the encouragement and confidence to believe he was on the right track.

In 1942 he established Tom Clark Confections. My mother, my father, and I worked in every aspect of the business, producing, packaging, and marketing a variety of confections for clients in California and across the United States. I did everything from cracking eggs into a mixing bowl as a toddler to taking phone orders after school. My younger brother, Tommy, began working in the family business during his high school years.

When the Second World War broke out, Tom Clark Confections grew at a breakneck speed. My father landed a contract with the U.S. Armed Forces Post Exchange (PX) stores, and Hollywood celebrities began to place special orders for elaborate trays of sweets that my mother designed. The entire family and all the employees put in many, many long hours to make sure all orders were filled perfectly.

Tom Clark making fruitcakes

My father suffered a stroke in 1974 and lingered until his death in 1980. By that time my brother, Tommy, was fully entrenched in running the business and raising his children, Tom Jr., Tim, Janie, and Karen, with his wife, Beverly. Following Beverly's death, Tommy retired and now enjoys a life of golf and travels with his friend, Donna Warren. Tom Clark Confections is still a successful business and is now in the hands of a third generation, Tommy's sons.

Throughout my youth, I continued to sing in churches, on KMPC radio, and at special local events, very often with the Beverly Hill Billies, whom I mentioned earlier. The Beverly Hill Billies were called "the most noted of all Southern California radio entertainers" and were often featured at the Angelus Temple in Los Angeles. I particularly loved the gospel songs we sang that had congregations stomping their feet and clapping wildly to our lively music. As much as I loved singing, when I became older and our family's livelihood no longer depended on my appearances, I began to devote less and less time to music. There was the war, and there were boys!

The Universal Braille Press that I visited as a child evolved into Braille Institute of America, and in 1971 they opened their first regional center in Anaheim, California. The institute is a nonprofit organization mostly funded through private donations. It provides a variety of free services, classes, and programs for the visually impaired through its five centers and outreach classes held throughout Southern California.

In 1971 I enrolled as a student, and within a few weeks, I was a volunteer in their Speakers' Bureau. I was then hired as a coordinator of community services, and in that role I developed public education programs for primary and secondary school children, college students, and adults. I also spoke to many service organizations and clubs with the message that people with disabilities come from all walks of life, all ages, and all races. Most strive to live independent and productive lives as contributing members in their communities.

My speaking engagements took me all over California and the United States. It just so happened that a very special guest was at a Rotary meeting in Los Angeles. I gave my talk, and up walked the president of Rotary International. "Betty," he said, "I enjoyed your talk, and I would like to invite you to come to London, England, to speak at our Rotary International Annual Convention, all expenses paid."

I remember gasping and thinking, *Oh my gosh! I am going to Europe!*

In 1984 I addressed the seven-hundred-member London Rotary Club at the Café Royal on Regents Street in London. It was a wonderful experience. Virginia went with me, and before returning to the United States, we toured England and made another trip to France.

My job also provided me with opportunities to meet and befriend many new people. One aspect of my work that was particularly interesting was serving as a technical consultant for writers, actors, and directors who were producing stage plays, television programs, or feature films in which a visually impaired character was portrayed. It was important for the actors' interpretation of a blind person to be accurate and believable. I worked with the producers and actors on many TV series, including *Little House on the Prairie* and *Love Boat. TV Guide* reported Victoria Principal's three-day, blindfolded training with me in preparation for her TV movie *Blind Rage.* I also worked with Laura Dern in *Mask,* a full-feature film, with Linda Purl in the television miniseries *Pompeii,* and with Jack Lemon, Ray Bradbury, Patty Duke, Jack Nicholson, and many more.

Jack Nicholson was a favorite of mine, and we really hit it off. He was a darling, so when I heard he was having a book signing in Palm Springs, Stu and I drove down to see him. I wasn't sure if he would remember me, but when we walked in the door, I heard him bellow, "Betty Clark!" Stu said Jack nearly jumped over the table. He ran up and gave me an unforgettable hug. I have always loved that man!

I also have always had a very active social life. I have enjoyed entertaining and cooking for my family and friends and going to the movies and theater and musical events. I was game to try just about anything, and sometimes opportunities to learn new things sprang up at work.

My office was in the Braille Institute Headquarters in Los Angeles, and every once in a while a class was offered in the building that would grab my attention. One was a square dancing class.

A popular, twenty-two-year-old, internationally known square dance caller named Marlin Hull had offered to volunteer his time and expertise to develop a program that would produce dancers that would be able to rival any square dancers anywhere. I could not resist and enrolled immediately. Soon there were eight of us, just enough for a square, all with significant vision loss and all eager students.

Marlin quickly learned that he needed to devise a way to demonstrate steps so we would know exactly what he wanted us to do. He became very good at giving us concise verbal instructions. He also taught us to use a silent cadence where each of us counted to ourselves to keep the right number of beats for each call. Marlin was an excellent teacher and taught us intricate steps that put us right up there with seasoned dancers.

Each of us in the group also belonged to local square dance clubs to get extra practice, so we were not only dancing with each other but with sighted dancers as well. It was really fun, and the more we practiced, the better we got—good enough to go on the road with our show. We traveled all over California as the Braille Institute Exhibition Square Dancers. We were so good, in fact, that some audiences would not believe we were visually limited. They were astonished at our dancing skills, and we were proud of being able to share our abilities. At the end of each performance, I gave a short speech about the programs and services Braille Institute offered.

Braille Institute's Exhibition Square Dancers
with Betty in the forefront.

Another momentous occasion for the Braille Institute Exhibition Square Dancers was when we were invited to perform at the arrival of the Freedom Train at the Anaheim Stadium in January of 1976. The Freedom Train was a twenty-six car, steam engine, locomotive-powered train that toured all forty-eight contiguous states during the American bicentennial. Ten of the cars held an exhibit of over five hundred artifacts that represented the two-hundred-year history of our nation. When the train stopped, communities held welcoming celebrations and programs. Millions of people toured the train's exhibits, and millions more lined the tracks as the Freedom Train passed by. Astronaut Buzz Aldrin, Johnny Cash, Debbie Reynolds, Mickey Mouse, and the Disney marching band, along with a host of politicians, celebrities, and local citizens, all joined in the festivities. The Braille Institute Exhibition Square Dancers were asked to perform during the Anaheim celebrations, and it was the most joyful, patriotic, pride-inspiring event we had experienced.

All in all, we performed for nearly six years, and when the group finally disbanded, we knew we had done something amazing, not only for Braille Institute and our audiences but also for ourselves.

Another class that caught my eye was weaving. All the threads and yarns fascinated me. I was amazed that such beautiful fabrics could be produced on the large looms, so I decided to enroll. Soon I was making my own fabrics and then designing clothing. I took to weaving as a fish takes to water and enjoyed it so much that Ted bought me a wonderful sixteen-harness, twelve-treadle loom to have at home. Weaving was a wonderful way to unwind after work.

I think I surprised myself and everyone else when I began to enter my designs into various competitions and began to win. I won over thirty prizes, twenty of them blue ribbons, at the Los Angeles County Fair in Pomona, the Southern California Exposition at Del Mar, the Southern Conference of California Handweavers, and other events. I was even offered a job designing fabric for an exclusive Arizona designer that I felt I must politely decline.

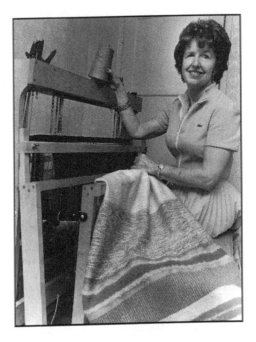

Betty at her Loom

I had several opportunities to model my own work. One was at the Beau James Fashion Extravaganza, a fund-raiser for Braille Institute held at the Riviera Hotel in Palm Springs. I rehearsed walking down the runway over and over again, with Beau James coaching my every step so my gait would be smooth and natural. I was a bit nervous about the possibility of losing my orientation and falling off the runway, but he assured me there would be people on both sides of the runway to make sure that didn't happen.

The Extravaganza drew a full house, and many models wearing the latest fashions were waiting in the wings for the event to begin. When it came my turn, I stepped out on the runway in my hand-woven, silver-blue, metallic gown, not a soul in the audience knowing I had limited vision. I walked down the runway and back with not a stumble, trip, or fall. And when I heard the round of applause, I was so relieved and very happy.

Of all my weaving projects, my most ambitious was weaving the American flag with every one of the thirteen stripes and fifty stars. The flag was about four feet long by two and a half feet wide. The red stripes were of mohair threads, the white stripes were of metallic wool, and the blue field was also of metallic wool. I enlisted the help of my mother to cut the white stars from a large, woven, white metallic wool piece and help me hand-stitch them into place.

In 1976, during our country's centennial celebration, I had the great honor of presenting that flag as a gift to First Lady Betty Ford, the wife of our thirty-eighth president, Gerald R. Ford. The White House set up a news conference in Burbank.

I was escorted into a hangar at the Burbank Airport and seated in a roped-off area. The press was directly in front of me, and we all waited as Air Force One landed and taxied up to the door of the hangar. Mrs. Ford exited the plane, came up to a podium and microphone, welcomed everyone, and then asked, "Is Betty Clark here?" I stood, was introduced, and was escorted to the podium, where Mrs. Ford said, "I hear you have something for me." I greeted her with a few words and presented her with the flag. She was so gracious and appreciative, and I was very humbled by her kindness.

When I got home, I excitedly told Ted about my day. "Oh, Ted, I wish you could have been there. It was really wonderful."

"I was there, Betty," he said quietly. "I was given clearance and was standing just to the left of where you were sitting."

"What?! Why didn't you tell me?" I said with a groan.

"Because, darling, it was your day, and I did not want to be any kind of distraction for you. You were wonderful." It was another moment when I was so grateful to have Ted in my life.

On July 1, 1976, I received the following on White House stationary:

Dear Betty,

It was such a pleasure to meet you during my trip to California, and I want to thank you once again for the beautifully hand-woven flag. How proud I am to add it to my memorabilia! Your courage and determination must be an inspiration to all who know you, and I shall always cherish this gift and the friendship of the exceptional woman who made it. All the Fords join in sending warm best wishes.

Sincerely, Betty Ford

I met Nancy Reagan, the wife of our fortieth president, Ronald Reagan, when she attended a building dedication at Braille Institute in Los Angeles. During the dedication program, the Braille Institute Exhibition Square Dancers performed, and immediately following I presented Mrs. Reagan with a multi-color wool shawl I had woven. She was very grateful to receive it, and once again I felt humbled to be able to share an example of my work with her. I was also grateful for the opportunity to express my gratitude and appreciation for all the tireless work and attention Mrs. Reagan gave to our country in her unique and gracious manner.

First Lady, Nancy Reagan and Betty

Working is something I have always relished; even from the time I was three. I was blessed with skills, abilities, and a positive attitude that made work enjoyable, and I was very much aware of the rewards of my efforts. Of course, the money was nice, but it was the adventure, the friendships, the independence, and the contributions I was able to make along the way that have made me so deeply grateful for all my employment experiences. I have never regretted one moment I put in at the office.

15

SENSITIVITY AND GOOD SENSE

Sensitivity and good sense is a little catchphrase that popped into my head years ago and became the title for a philosophy and for methods of interacting effectively with all kinds of people. It is something I am deeply, deeply passionate about because it encompasses my life's work and the reason for this book. So if you will bear with me....

I have shared stories of my life as illustrations of how I have lived very much like anyone else. I have had blessings and tragedies. I have had loves and losses. I worked and played. I learned by guidance and the hard way. And even though I have spent my life as an inspirational and motivational speaker, there are many, many lessons I have had to learn myself. Maintaining hope, learning trust, nurturing faith, living a balanced life, developing patience, and being tolerant of other ways of living, thought, and belief are the foundations of sensitivity and good sense.

Betty taking notes with a braille slate and stylus

In my mind, sensitivity is awareness and enlightenment. Good sense is how you respectfully put sensitivity into action. True sensitivity is learned, the same as hatred and discrimination are often passed down from one generation to the next. What we learn and do instinctively becomes part of our personality and beliefs. It is important to know how we come to this and why we are the way we are.

In a recent study, researchers showed photographs of individuals of various races, ethnic dress, disabilities, and ages to a diverse group of students. The students were asked, "Which person in this group of photos would you trust?" Inevitably, the students chose a person who had one or more of the same traits they did. They were asked to choose a photo of someone they would not trust or who made them uncomfortable. The students most often chose photos of people who were the most different from them. The researchers concluded that we instinctively choose likeness as a protective action. It is only with exposure to those who are different in some way that we begin to discover that there are some universal likenesses, and it is from these that we can begin to develop understanding. This is how we overcome the fear of differences and embrace similarities.

When I was in my early teens, I became very curious about religion. I grew up in a Seventh-day Adventist household and had been singing in Protestant Christian churches since I was three years old. Most of the churches were similar, with a preacher, elders, choir, offerings, communion, hymnals, and pews. Several of these churches believed that to receive God's grace, everyone must follow only their religious doctrine. Those who did not follow their specific beliefs were *not* going to get into heaven.

I talked with my friend Virginia about this. "How," I asked her, "do we know which of these churches' beliefs are the true path to glory?" It was very perplexing. We did not have an answer, so we decided the best way to determine which faith to follow would be to visit a different house of worship every week.

Virginia had a car and a driver's license, so we began our quest to find the one true church of God. We started by visiting a Catholic church, then the next week a Buddhist temple, followed by a charismatic church, a Jewish temple, a Mormon church, an Islamic mosque, and a couple of churches where we could not discern exactly what they believed or who they were. Sometimes we were only allowed in a visitors' area, but mostly we were welcome to participate as their parishioners did.

We went to the high desert near Joshua Tree, California, and sat in a tepee where spiritual services were being held and a pipe was being passed. We heard a talk by Manly P. Hall, the founder of the Philosophical Research Society, who was known as a leading scholar in the fields of religion, mythology, mysticism, and the occult. And we delved into the quatrains of fifteenth-century seer Nostradamus. No stone that we could find was left unturned.

I realize now, of course, that it was very ambitious for two naïve teenaged girls to think they could hone down the mysteries of centuries of religious activity. The houses of worship we visited held extensive histories, diverse cultural traditions, and complex and conflicting theologies we could not have possibly absorbed in just a few visits. Even so, that adventure became one of the most profound experiences of my life. I discovered that in every house of worship we entered, there were two common themes. One was love for a higher power and/or love for humankind. The second was the desire to find a path for a better life here on earth, in the afterlife, or both.

What surprised us most were the things we liked in nearly every house of worship we visited. In most cases, the people were generous and kind. Also, to my surprise, the experience brought to the forefront the lessons my parents had taught me about tolerance, acceptance, and sensitivity toward other beliefs, cultures, and people. Then there were the two things Virginia and I now knew for sure. First, that everyone should learn about as many religions and philosophies as possible to decide which fits best. Second, anyone can go to church and go through the required rituals and still be an insensitive jerk. Our self-guided adventure and research led to an acceptance of and sensitivity to beliefs other than the ones we knew growing up.

Another effective way to build sensitivity is by creating opportunities for young people to experience how people with low vision live. I gave this quite a bit of thought and organized the YES (Youth Engaged in Service) Conference at Braille Institute in Rancho Mirage, California. High school students from various youth service groups, such as Rotary Interact, the Lions LEO Club, Kiwanis Key Clubs, the Optimists, and Soroptimist Clubs were invited to a day of classes at Braille Institute, including adaptive cooking, independent living, sensory awareness, orientation and mobility, braille, and computer activities.

The students were divided into groups and rotated between the classes. At lunch I spoke briefly with them and, at the end of the day, we discussed their experiences. The positive evaluations of their new experiences were just what we had hoped for. It was heartwarming to see the students' enthusiasm and understanding of not only how people with low vision adapt to live normal lives but the importance of the YES program itself as a way to promote understanding.

It truly is confounding to me that both children and adults are often judged entirely by the way they look. Yet I know it is true because I am frequently complimented on my appearance, often with great surprise.

People are astounded that I do my own hair and make-up. On my daily checklist are brush teeth; style hair; apply subtle makeup; put on clean, stylish clothes; slip into shined shoes; and add tasteful accessories. This is how many workingwomen prepare for their day, and

I am no different. When they ask how I do it, I jokingly respond, "Much easier than you. I don't have to use a mirror."

I learned early on that always looking my best opens doors for me, because that is the way the sighted world works. It is totally irrelevant to me what color or size a person is, and what they are wearing is even less important. What is important to me is a person's attitude, warmth, and sensitivity to the needs of others, as well as the sincerity in his or her voice and the kindness in his or her heart. My superficial appearance is something I can change to gain that positive first impression. What I and everyone else cannot change is the color of our skin.

In late August of 1965, I had a date to speak to a Rotary group in the Watts neighborhood of Los Angeles. Rotary was just one of many different types of groups I addressed. There were students, church groups, service groups, medical organizations, and university groups. I usually began with my life story, the services and programs Braille Institute offered, and the need for public education on interacting respectfully and effectively with people with disabilities. I have always kept my talks upbeat and positive and ended them with an audience-appropriate quote. I learned by experience not to take questions at the close of my talk but to offer to address questions during the mingle time at the end of the program. Often the questions asked would change the focus of the points I had just made. I wanted to leave each member of my audience with a positive frame of mind and a better understanding of the topic at hand. The formula always worked well, and I enjoyed many, many speaking engagements.

I was looking forward to meeting the Watts Rotary group because I had not visited them in the past. However, just days before my scheduled talk, riots had broken out in the area, leaving thirty-six dead, hundreds injured, and millions of dollars of damage. The riots began with the drunk-driving arrest of an African American man by white police officers. A struggle ensued, and neighbors began to gather to watch. The area had been under great social and racial tension, and this incident, on a hot summer's night, was all it took for the crowd to get out of hand and a riot to break out. When it was over five days later, the Watts area looked like an enormous bomb had exploded in the middle of the neighborhood.

As the date approached for my speech, I booked a car to take me to the Rotary meeting. "Betty, you can't go," my friends protested. "It is far too dangerous." I remembered the many times my parents had stepped up to do the right thing and decided I had no choice but to go. I had a very gracious invitation and a job to do, and there would be a group of people expecting me to be there as promised.

On the day of my appointment, I rode through Los Angeles and into Watts with no problem, and the meeting went smoothly. Afterward a man from the audience approached me and thanked me for coming. He told me that he was from the local NAACP (National Association for the Advancement of Colored People) and wondered if I would like to speak at their next meeting. I said, "Of course."

"You are one brave little lady to be here today, and I look forward to introducing you to our group and hearing you speak," he said.

The truth was, I was honored because I knew there was still great tension in the community, and skin color was an issue on both sides. Their acceptance of the messages during my speech and of me personally was endearing.

From there I was invited to speak at a meeting of the Benevolent Protective Order of the Black Elks. I had never heard of the Black Elks and learned it was formed in 1899. As with most fraternal organizations during that era, African Americans were denied membership, so they formed their own organization to provide financial, spiritual, and emotional support within their communities.

*Betty spoke to many groups and organizations
up until a few weeks before her death.*

Once again, I appreciated the group's positive comments at the end of my talk, and I felt as if I had a whole new circle of friends. Before I left the meeting,

I was asked to ride in their lead car in an upcoming parade in Los Angeles. Now, what lady could refuse to ride through the streets of one of America's finest cities on a sunny Southern California day, in a shiny new convertible with friends?

16

TRIPS WITHIN THE JOURNEY

Life is a journey filled with side trips!
I have always loved traveling, whether it is around the corner or around the globe. It is simply impossible for me to pass up an opportunity to experience new places and meet new people.

My first trip abroad was not very long after the Second World War. My friend Jeannie and I decided to go to Paris because, to us, it was the most romantic and chic city in the world. I longed to see the fashions, taste the food, climb the Eiffel Tower, and sit in an outdoor café, devouring oven-fresh rolls with steaming cups of coffee.

Jeannie and I bought airline tickets and flew from Los Angeles to New York and then to Paris. We took a cab to our hotel, checked in, and fell into bed. Despite being exhausted from the trip the day before, we were up early the next morning. We couldn't wait to explore the city.

The hotel suggested we visit a restaurant famous for its pastries that was just a few blocks away. We used a tourist map the hotel provided as a guide to find our way there. After many left turns and right turns, we realized we were hopelessly lost. A woman passing by saw us looking at the map and began to speak to us in French. Neither Jeannie nor I spoke French, so we just pointed to the name of the restaurant that was written on the map. The woman's eyes lit up, and she motioned for us to follow her. She took us four blocks—right to the door of the restaurant. We were so grateful, and as I reached into my purse, she put her hand on mine, smiled, and said, "No, no." And away she went. I have never forgotten her kindness and other acts of generosity from the French people during our stay.

At this time I had about 2 percent vision. I could see light, shadows, and color. Though I could not see, I could touch, smell, hear, and feel the movement and the mood of the environment around me. The idea that people with limited vision develop super-powered hearing is just a myth. My other senses have never been any greater than anyone else's. I just relied on my sensory perception differently than most people do. So despite my limited vision, I have always enjoyed travel just as much as most anyone else would.

Jeannie and I returned to Los Angeles ten days later with lots of memories. In our suitcases we each had a genuine article of French clothing and a bottle of authentic French perfume, which were the envy of our girlfriends. I loved every minute I spent in Paris, and for years I daydreamed about going back again someday—maybe with a gentleman I loved.

Another place I had always wanted to visit was St. Petersburg, Russia. A couple of years later, Jeannie and I packed our bags again and were off to the Communist country. We flew to Moscow and boarded a river cruise ship that took us to see all the sights of the two Russian capitals: the political capital, Moscow, and St. Petersburg, the cultural and artistic capital. The military presence was everywhere. Each time we got off the ship, we had to be cleared. Armed soldiers lined each side of the gangplanks as we disembarked. One by one we went through a turnstile and were escorted up to a desk, where we presented our passports. Our passports were collected, and we were issued a small red book that we were to keep with us until we returned to the ship. Only then were our passports returned to us.

St. Petersburg looks like a city you might read about in a fairytale book. The colorful, extravagant palace-like architecture of the Hermitage, St. Isaac's Cathedral, and Mariinsky Theatre was more than one could possibly imagine.

There were about twenty of us in our tour group, and even though it was a Communist country and the

Cold War was not too far behind us, we felt safe walking through the cities. Our tour guides were friendly and accommodating. Once they were aware of my limited vision, they bent the rules and allowed me to touch some of the art objects on display.

In 1958 a book was published called *The Ugly American;* it is about an insensitive, boorish American diplomat assigned to a fictitious Asian country. This character loosely defined the stereotypical loud, obnoxious, demanding American tourists in the years that followed. It seemed we had a real live "ugly American" as part of our tour group in Russia. Our fellow tourist had been complaining about this and that all through the trip. As our group toured a museum in St. Petersburg, he became more agitated than usual, and we all began to keep our distance from him.

He finally erupted into full-blown rage at one of the tour guides, who was describing the creation of a particular work of art and how it related to the political history of Russia. Our ugly American shouted, "This is just a bunch of propaganda, and I am not going listen to it anymore." An argument began between him, the tour guide, and the museum security.

As you might imagine, our entire group was quickly ushered out of the museum and given a military escort back to the ship. Everyone in the group was embarrassed. We were also angry with this man, with his behavior, and with having our tour cut short because of his nasty outburst. We went back to the dock to retrieve our passports and board the ship. The same man who had collected my passport hours before leaned over, placed my passport in my hand, and whispered, "I like you very much. Please come back again." Somehow those kind words relieved the pain of having to leave early.

Stu and I made the same trip again years later. I was shocked by the difference between pre- and post-Communist Russia. The sense of safety was gone. People soliciting money constantly approached us. Prices had gone through the roof, and polite service was a thing of the past. Even so, this did not dampen my appreciation of the people, culture, history, and art of Russia.

Al, my first husband, and I worked at Tom Clark Confections together before and after we were married. Every year we took a trip to Northern California with his Portuguese American family. Al's family lived in the San Joaquin Valley of California, where they grew fruit and olives. They were hard workers and looked forward to the annual trip north to recharge before the next growing season. Usually about eighteen to twenty family members would pile into a large rented house for two weeks of endless eating and fun. We panned for gold, drove to the Reno casinos that were only an hour away, and joined in the local summer activities. The Holy Ghost Celebration in Oakley, California, was an event we never missed. It was a celebration to honor the thirteenth-century charitable Queen Isabella, who stole bread from the palace to feed the poor. The king caught her with bread bundled up in her apron and demanded that she drop her apron. When she did, a miracle happened. The bread disappeared, and rose petals fell to the floor.

A processional parade led by a costumed young woman representing Queen Isabella traveled through the streets of Oakley to St. Anthony's Catholic Church. There everyone received a traditional Portuguese meal of fresh-baked bread and a beef soup called sopa. It was a tradition I enjoyed for many years.

Ted and I traveled mostly around Southern California and to Nevada on occasion. His film work involved quite a bit of travel, so when he returned home, he wanted a rest from all the planes, trains, and film-equipment trucks. But we never felt deprived, because there was always something exciting and fun to do just minutes from our home in Los Angeles.

Stu loved travel as much as I did. We took our first international trip together to Cancun, Mexico. The Spanish invasion and the demise of the Mayan population captured his imagination, so we decided we had to go and do some exploring on our own. We flew down to Cancun, hired a private guide, and visited all the pre-Columbian historical sites and tourist attractions. Stu had a video camera and filmed everything. He decided he wanted to go deep into the forests with another guide, and I gladly sent him off with his cameras while our guide and I went to see the sights of the city. Both of us had a terrific day.

One afternoon Stu and I were walking through a park in Cancun when two little girls in starched, white, embroidered dresses began to watch us. They were very curious about the way Stu was assisting me as we walked, and they wanted to try being my guide. The girls got on either side of me and took my hands to walk with me. The language differences made it difficult for them to tell me if a step was in front of me and if it was a step up or a step down. Stu quickly rescued me, and the girls gave me farewell hugs and then skipped off, hand in hand, through the park. They were so adorable, and I enjoyed the encounter immensely, even though I had worried about my safety for a moment.

We also visited the city of Merida in southern Mexico, and it was there that I had the best margarita of my life. We enjoyed horse-and-buggy rides to and from restaurants and often visited a little mall where we would have a drink and listen to live music.

Our guide invited us to visit his home and meet his family. This took us off the tourist track and gave us the opportunity to experience another view of Mexican life. The family was warm and welcoming, and we were deeply grateful for their generosity. By the time we returned to Cancun, the Gulf War had broken out, and we were advised by the American embassy to return to the United States. So we were forced to cut our trip short and returned home.

Stu decided he would like to return to France and show me all the places he had lived and worked. It was amazing how many things in Paris felt completely different with Stu. It seemed livelier, brighter, and lovelier. We ate boxed lunches in view of the Eiffel Tower while nearby a woman in a black shawl played an accordion. We strolled along the Rive Gauche (Left Bank), which is where philosophers, artists, and writers gathered and lived as an internationally recognized creative community years ago. (Stu particularly loved this area of the city because of his background in art and history.)

And on this trip a French woman shared with me one of the secrets of being Parisian. She said, "You must learn the art and experience the joy of doing absolutely nothing." It is not my nature to do nothing. It was an entirely new concept to me because I always thought of doing absolutely nothing as being lazy. I was eager to give it a try while in Paris, so Stu and I would go to the parks around Paris and do absolutely nothing. It takes more practice than one might think!

Stu and I enjoyed taking cruises. We traveled to several countries that way, including Spain, Portugal, Malta, Holland, Scandinavia, and Panama.

The Panama Canal cruise was one of the most memorable. The ship was luxurious, the food was fantastic, and the service was wonderful. When we arrived in Panama, we decided to take advantage of the onshore adventures. Stu always liked to get away from the tourist areas and explore the "real" country.

Eiffel Tower, Paris France

One offering was an overnight package to a small village a couple of hours outside Panama. We were given a guide with a jeep-like vehicle that he drove with great enthusiasm. He drove us to our hotel, where we checked in and left our luggage in our room. Then we started on a tour of historical sites in the area. Stu noticed storm clouds gathering and asked the guide about the changing weather. The guide said, "Oh, don't worry. It never rains for very long here."

And with that the skies opened up, and it poured down rain like we had never seen before or since. After about an hour of waiting out the storm in the vehicle, we decided it would be best to return to the hotel. As we drove up to the hotel entrance, the wind began to blow so strongly that I had a hard time staying on my feet. I clung to Stu as we made our way through the doors. We stood in the lobby, wet to the bone, took a couple of deep breaths, and made our way to our room on the second floor. Stu unlocked the door, and we were met with a blast of rain that hit us like flying needles.

"Stu," I shouted over the roaring wind, "close the window!"

"I can't," he answered.

"Please try, Stu. I am freezing. Close the window."

"There is no window."

"What? I can feel the rain coming into the room, Stu. Please try again."

"Betty, there is a hole in the wall but no glass or shutters."

"Are you kidding me? Call the lobby."

We called the lobby and asked for another room, but none was available. We then asked for a ride back to the ship. The road was washed out, and they could not get us back until morning. How about dry bedding? None available. So we had no choice but to lie on top of a soggy bed and wait until morning. I remember thinking; *This is the end of the world.* But it wasn't, and years later we laughed about the Panama cruise being the most memorable of all our trips.

These trips have been part of my larger life journey. My journey—my life—has *not* been about blindness. It has been about taking the necessary steps to adapt to the world around me so I can fully enjoy the opportunities and relationships that make being alive a rich, full experience. It has been about having the vision, the courage and the faith to take each next step of the journey.

$\mathcal{E}$ P I L O G U E

$\mathcal{I}$n 2006 Stu and Betty Mong were driving home from a medical conference in Palm Springs, California, where Betty had been speaking. It was a beautiful morning and the rush-hour traffic had thinned. They chatted about being grateful that they no longer faced the frustrations and dangers of Los Angeles traffic. They drove down the palm-tree lined Highway 111 toward Rancho Mirage and moved into the left-hand lane as Stu prepared to make a turn onto Country Club Drive.

They never saw it coming. In a split second, their car was hit broadside by another vehicle and hurtled across the street, where it slammed into a palm tree. The Jaws of Life was needed to pull them from the wreckage. Stu suffered severe head injuries, and Betty was in coma with a broken neck and back. They were hospitalized in separate specialized units because their injuries were medically very different.

Betty was in intensive care and was not allowed visitors, but a hospital chaplain devised a plan to sneak Stu in for a few brief visits. Hearing Stu's voice made all the difference in the world as Betty made her way out of a coma and back to being fully conscious.

Their injuries were so severe, they never fully recovered from that terrible accident. For the next four years, their lives were filled with doctor visits and physical therapy. Betty and Stu did resume many activities and social events with family and friends, but later Stu's health took a turn for the worse.

Betty and Stu Photo Credit: Janel Pahl

Stu passed away on February 19, 2012, and Betty was inconsolable. She would say, "My angel, my Stuie, is gone." Friends and family joined together to celebrate his life and their friend Howlett Smith came from Los Angles to serenade them with "You Never Let Me Down" and "As Time Goes By" one last time.

Betty went back to work speaking to various groups about her experiences and philosophies. She also threw herself into "the book"—this book. Everyone within hearing distance knew about "the book." Occasionally phone calls would come in while she and I were working. She would answer and say, "I can't talk now. I am working on the book," and then slam down the phone. She would tell me often that this book kept her engaged and gave her the unrelenting drive to go on as long as she could. Age and illness were stronger forces than her will, and she began to lose her battle. It was during this time that Betty became completely enamored with Pope Francis. Learning of his wisdom and kindness and hearing him speak on television gave her the spiritual comfort she sought for so many years. "He will change the world", she told me.

On November 9, 2013, the last day of her life, I had a few minutes alone with Betty in her hospital room. Her personal assistant, Roger, who had been at her side in the hospital for the past five days and nights, had gone to the nurse's station to take care of some administrative duties.

We all knew the end was near, and as I sat beside her bed, I suddenly didn't know what to say or do. She was no longer speaking and barely responding. I took her hand in mine. It was warm and soft. I watched her for a moment. I wondered if I should say it was OK to go? I didn't know if I had the right to say those words. It seemed like shoving her out the door somehow. Then I remembered I had a manuscript of this book in my bag.

I opened the manuscript with the intention of reading her favorite parts to her. So I chose the chapter where she first met Stu. As I began to read, her head turned ever so slightly toward me, and there was a momentary light squeeze to my hand. I was suddenly completely overwhelmed by a deep sadness that left me struggling to catch my breath. My eyes filled with blinding tears, and my voice cracked as I tried to continue reading.

I was so angry with myself. She was bravely facing death, and I was quickly becoming a blubbering mess. I needed to be strong and comforting for her, so I struggled to pull myself together as quickly as I could. I continued reading, though my throat was so painfully constricted the words could only squeeze through in a whisper. Soon Roger and the nurses returned. I put her story safely back in my bag along with the promise to look after it in the years to come. In less than an hour, she was gone.

***

Betty asked that the following words be her final in this book: "My last wish, and the only gift of real value I have left to give, is to share my story with you, dear readers, to remind you that no matter what your obstacles, you *can* turn your vision into a dream come true. No excuses. And the best time to begin is *now!*"

With love, Betty

***

Made in the USA
San Bernardino, CA
15 November 2017